The Competency Question Book for Job Interviews

Mike New

Revised 3rd edition

Previously published as The Competency Question Handbook

To my mother,
to whom I owe everything

Some material in this book also
appears in The Civil Service
Competencies Book

CONTENTS

Chapter 1   What is a competency ?

1.1   Competence

A competency is simply a skill or an ability to do something efficiently. Giving good service to a customer is a competency. Showing attention to detail is another.

Years ago, interviewers asked about your school or qualifications. Then, there was a fashion for 'situational interviewing', in which candidates would be told a situation and asked to imagine how they would react to it. An example that you might have been given is "Imagine that you are working in an office and you receive a phone call in which the caller tells you that there is a bomb in your building . How would you react to it ? "   Or "Imagine that one of your work colleagues tells you that he fiddles his expenses account. What would you do ?"

Nowadays, however, interviewers have moved away from that type of interviewing because psychologists told them that competency interviewing is a better guide to how we would perform in any job. It is believed that our past behaviour is a much more accurate guide to our future behaviour and therefore many more companies have now adopted the competency approach.

1.2   How competency interviews work

In a competency interview, you will be asked about your experiences. You will be asked to provide examples of how you performed particular tasks. So, if the job involves working with customers in any way, you could be asked to give an example of how you have delivered excellent customer satisfaction or perhaps how you have dealt with an irate or demanding customer. If the job involves cash-handling, you might well be asked to give an example of when you have demonstrated attention to detail or integrity.

Most current interviews last around 30 minutes and you can expect to be asked about three or four competency questions. Each question will invite you to give an example of how you have used that skill in the past and each answer should last about 3 minutes. It is important that you answer in a certain way. You must describe a particular situation or problem that needed resolving, then the action you took to resolve it and finally what the positive outcome and benefits were to you and others.

1.3   The advantages to you of competency interviews

In a later chapter, I shall be showing you how it is possible to predict some of the probable questions in the interview. So, one advantage is that you can **prepare your answers in advance**. Many people hated the old situational interviews, where you were suddenly given a hypothetical scenario and asked to imagine what you would do. Often, jobseekers had never encountered that situation before in their lives and the experience was really stressful. Thankfully, those types of interviews are rare now.

As well as being able to prepare your answers, you can **practise them** over and over again.

These interviews give you the opportunity to really sell your talents and your worth to an employer. If you have actually done the job before or done the task that you are being asked about, then the employer is often **willing to overlook any lack of qualifications** that you may have. Employers are now more interested in what you have **done**, not who you are or how much you have managed to memorise for exams. George Osborne was the Chancellor of the Exchequer, running the economy of this country and in charge of trillions and yet he didn't even have a GCSE in Economics or Business Studies. This point is very important and I shall be saying a lot more about this later.

Another great advantage is that, unless the interviewer specifically asks you for an example from work, you can relate **an example from any sphere of your life**. It might be a group you are involved in or some voluntary work you once did or some experience you once had while on holiday. This is very important and I shall be saying a lot more about this in the next chapter.

So, to those who dread competency interviews, I say : ' Have no fear ! ' From now on, I want you to change your mindset and to see them in a totally different light. You must see them as glorious opportunities. If you follow the guidelines and are willing to work hard, you will be in a much better position and actually look forward to showcasing your skills at such interviews.

Summary of advantages to the jobseeker :

- You can prepare your answers in advance

- You can practise your answers

- You can sell your talents and worth , even if you might not have the required qualifications

- You can use examples from outside of work

1.4   Competency-based application forms

These too are becoming more common and more employers are using them as a way of sifting out candidates. Sometimes, literally hundreds of people apply for just a handful of jobs. Naturally, they cannot all be invited for an interview and increasingly employers are using this method to determine which applicants can demonstrate that they already have the required skills. It saves the employer expensive training costs.

Competency questions on applications forms are an excellent opportunity to sell yourself and to convince the employer that you are the solution to his business needs. Moreover, you are not under the pressure of an interview when completing the form. You can do it at your leisure. From now on, I want you to be positive about these type of application forms because we will now be examining how you can much more easily complete them, once you have built up your personal Experiences Autobiography.

Occasionally, the application process will involve selecting answers from given Competency Options. I will deal with this in Chapter 11.

1.5   If you are applying for Civil service jobs

The Civil Service has some competencies, which are quite unlike the mainstream competencies outlined in this book. You will need my other book 'The Civil Service Competencies Book', if you are applying for a job there.

Chapter 2   Doing an experience stocktake

2.1   The experience stocktake

One of the greatest difficulties that jobseekers face at competency interviews is that they cannot think of a specific occasion of when they have performed that task and cannot describe an example to demonstrate their skills in that area. It is highly frustrating for them because they know that they have carried out that action many times to a high standard before but cannot recall it on demand. They lose the job of their dreams. Is this you ?

To pre-empt this happening to you as much as you possibly can, you must make yourself aware of all the experiences you have had. To do this, I am going to get you to realise and recognise that you have many more skills than you may realise. I want you to do **an experience stocktake.**

Sofia worked in a call-centre. I asked her to list her duties. She replied: " *I just answered incoming calls from people who had seen ads in papers, took their details and arranged for info to be sent out to them* ".

Actually, what she did was to deliver excellent customer service in a friendly and professional manner by taking incoming calls. She would use her great communication skills to actively listen and communicate appropriately and sometimes employ her persuasion and business acumen skills to sell additional items. She would use her time management skills to control talkative callers and meet her targets and use her negotiation skills and problem-solving skills to sort out any callers who phoned in with complaints. She often exchanged her shift days with colleagues, showing her teamwork nature. She would log the confidential details of callers onto the inhouse software, while still actively listening, demonstrating her multi-tasking ability and IT skills.

Can you see that while Sofia thought that she only answered calls, took details and arranged for items to go out, she actually has a broad range of skills that she can use as starting points for examples in an interview situation ? This is so typical. Most people do not realise that they have many skills until they are pointed out to them or are forced to sit and evaluate themselves.

2.2 List your duties in detail

Now comes the hard work. This chapter demands a great deal of work from you but I make no apology for that. Nothing in life is free. The rewards will be worth it.

If you are currently working, I want you to list what you did in your job last week, **in detail.** Every duty you had to perform, no matter how small or trivial it may seem. If last week was not a typical week because you were on a training course for example, then use a typical week. List all the people you liaised with, both inside your workplace and outside. List any incidents . List all the equipment / machinery you used. That is very important. List every function you performed, even the smallest.

Why ? Because every experience you have had could help you to land that job you seek. The purpose of this is to get you to ultimately see that **you have many more abilities than you realise** and have had many more experiences than you think.

Let me explain. Josh was an office worker and wondered at first why I was asking him to list the office machinery he used. It then prompted him to remember that the fax/ photocopier had a paperjam last week. That in turn reminded him about the time last year when he was alone because everyone was out to lunch and the fax/photocopier had jammed and he had a really urgent fax to send and how he was in a real mess. He decided not to panic.

He stayed calm and considered all his options. He thought about it for a few moments. He remembered that there was a manual in the fax drawer. He looked and found it wasn't there. He stayed calm and thought again. He copied down the name and model number of the machine, searched for it in Google, found the manual online, followed the trouble-shooting diagrams and quickly found the solution. So, he then realised that he *did* have problem-solving skills after all and had an example that he could use in any competency interview. He could also use that experience as an ' Initiative' example.

You must understand that all our experiences in life are important and that we forget most of them. Your task over the coming days and weeks is to try to remember those experiences and list them. From now on, you must get into the habit of recording your experiences in your **Experiences Autobiography**. More about that soon .

So, list every function that you performed last week in your job.

- Whom did you communicate with ? Inside/ outside the job.
- Did you work with others in any way ? Teamwork skills ?
- Did you perform a service of any kind whatsoever ?
- Did you have any deadlines or targets to meet ? Daily ? monthly ?
- Did you achieve anything ?
- Did you solve any problems ? Not a single one ?
- Did you organise anything ?
- Did you create anything ?
- Did you manage anything ?
- Did you improve, innovate, suggest something ?
- Did you show flexibility/ Adapt to changes / working practices ?
- Overcome setbacks or obstacles ?
- Did you negotiate ? Did you persuade ?
- Make major decisions ?
- Plan something ? Take responsibility for something ?
- Give a presentation ?
- Take the initiative ?
- Motivate someone ?
- Save the company any money or save waste ?
- Use ANY equipment ?

Think very slowly and carefully and take your time. This exercise must not be rushed or omitted. Don't be lazy. Invest time in this and you will be very surprised at what you find. A small experience can often spark a memory of something which can give you an excellent competency example for your interview.

If you do not have a job at the moment, then list all the things you did in your last two jobs. Remember to write down even the smallest thing you did. All the people you spoke to, inside and outside the company. All the equipment you used. All the incidents.

If you are a school-leaver or have never worked, no problem ! This next part applies to you too.

2.3   Now list every job you have ever done

Now comes the really hard work ! I want you to do the same for **all your previous** jobs. Yes, that's right, every single one. Seriously. Even if all your previous jobs have been in the same line of work, there will have been incidents that provide examples that can be used in your interview. The challenge now is for you to dig through your memory and exhume those long forgotten experiences and achievements. They can prove to be very valuable. The more time and effort you invest in remembering your past experiences, the far easier it will be to demonstrate your skills to an employer and land that dream job. It's that simple.

Ask your family and friends for help ! Ask you family, friends, partner, relatives and colleagues to remind you of all your previous jobs and things that have happened to you in the past. Log them all. For now, in no particular order.

2.4   List any of these achievements or activities :

School - Attended all year round - you never missed a day ? Head boy ? One of the house captains ? Any special responsibility ? In drama society ? In debating team ? In choir ? Best achiever of the Year ? Won the cross country county race ? Team sports captain ? It's unlikely that you would be asked to prove these by the interviewer but it will show the interviewer what type of person you are, what you achieved and can form the basis of other examples. Even being in the choir shows you can work in a team.

Scouts / Girl Guides / St John's Ambulance Brigade -Any notable achievements ? Have you raised any money for charity? Saved a life ?

Part-time jobs while at school Paper boy. Milk boy. Cleaner. Saturday job helping in a shop, yard, garage, market stall or farm. Note : no job is worthless. Every job is useful and has dignity and value, if done well, even the most humble.

Voluntary work or charity work - Have you shopped for the elderly ? Decorated an old folks' flat? Mowed their garden lawn ? Shovelled their snow away ? Raised money ? Looked after a pet ? Did a charity sponsored run/ marathon /walk ? Served in a second-hand shop ? Acted as a delivery driver for a charity shop ? Drive anyone home ? Served meals to the homeless at Christmas ? Handed out food at a food bank ? Organise a food bank ?

Community work Organised a fireworks party for your street ? Organised or helped to run any sort of community party / celebration / commemoration for your block of flats, street or community ? Acted as chairman, treasurer, minutes-taker or in any capacity in any neighbourhood watch / security scheme ? Act as a local spokesperson or representative ?

Church work   Have assisted in any way at your local church ? Helped organise or run annual fete ? Helped run the food bank ? Visited the elderly or sick ?

Local sports club   Washed their kit ?   Designed their leaflets ? Coached the kids ? Raised money for them ? Organised raffles bingos for them ? Worked in a team to clear snow off the pitch ?

Neighbours Solved disputes between them ? Done favours for them ? Communicated on their behalf ? Worked as a team with them ? Organised a street party or fireworks party ?

Local hospital - Ever helped them ? Attended their fete ? What happened ? Ever been a patient ? Made arrangements ? Visit the sick as a volunteer visitor ?

Local old cinema / concert hall - Ever tried to save it from closure ?

Olympic torch - Did you carry it ? What happened ?

In a hobbies club : chess, gardening. reading, inventing, computing, archery, cooking ? What happened ? Did you organise any competitions ? work as teams ? any accidents happen ? Resolve any problems or disputes ?

Travel experiences - see a crime ? negotiate a better deal ? have to change to a different hotel or airport ? get lost ? miss a flight ? give English lessons for free board or food ? prevent an accident ? had to hitch-hike ? get mugged or held up at gun-point ?

Health club / Gym Motivated yourself ? Lost weight ?

Evening-classes Taken courses to improve your skills ?

Driving test - any incidents ? make any sacrifices to pay for your lessons ?

Wedding - best man duties ? Had to give a speech ?

Holidays - planned any ? organised any ?

Family jobs with your children or nephews / nieces / grandchildren - Things you've done with kids : Organised birthday parties. Organised days out.

Any internships, work experience, placements, training courses, job-shadowing, school / uni coursework ?

Canvasser – ever work as a canvasser at election time ?

Dig out all your old payslips and diaries to remind you of your previous jobs. Find all certificates of achievements, accolades, awards, letters of promotion and qualifications. All of these are vital reminders of your experiences and skills.

A warning. If you have already compiled a CV, don't be tempted to think that your CV is sufficient and that you can omit the above exercise. A CV is merely a brief skeleton of your past. I want you to spend a good deal of time painstakingly reminding yourself of every single task you have ever done. If it takes you a week, then so be it. I cannot emphasise enough the importance of this exercise.

2.5   Building your Experiences Autobiography

The next step is to buy an A4 pad and a hard folder for it. On the front of the folder, write in a permanent black pen **'Experiences Autobiography'**. Alternatively, if you can afford to buy a large hardback notebook, whose pages have already been subdivided from A to Z, then so much the better.

The task now is to transfer your past experiences into your Experiences Autobiography by categorising them in a way which will assist you in getting your next job.

At the top of the page of your A4 pad, write the following competencies, one on each sheet :

- Adaptability to Change - Flexibility, Versatility
- Attention to Detail - Accuracy
- Communication Skills - Verbal or written, including phone Skills.
- Customer Service - Internal and external
- Deadlines, Targets and Achieving including Time Management
- Decision Making and Problem Solving
- Drive, Determination and Resilience, incl. self-motivation
- Initiative
- Leadership
- Negotiation, Persuasion , Influence and Motivating Others
- Teamwork / Collaborating / Partnering

You should have a separate sheet for each competency.

If you are using an A-Z notebook, obviously, you would enter *Teamwork* under T, both *Customer Service* and *Communication* under C (a separate page), *Decision Making* under D ,etc.

2.6 Logging your experiences into competencies

So, here is an example of how you must log all your past experiences into your Experience Autobiography file or book. Peter is an 18 year-old school-leaver who has not worked full-time but has remembered that he worked as a paper-boy and on one occasion, he noticed a man lying on the floor in his hallway.

He looked through the letter-box and realised that something was seriously wrong, went to the next-door neighbour and had him call an ambulance. His quick thinking saved that man's life. So, under the competency sheet headed **'Initiative'**, he writes ' Paperboy job – called ambulance'. That will remind him of that situation. While he was doing that job, he also had to interact with his customers, so he writes 'Paperboy job' on his **'Customer Service'** sheet. Same again for **'Communication** ' sheet.

When he was in the 6th form, he was part of a group that were given a day's instruction in decorating and then volunteered to decorate a pensioner's flat. They had to complete it in four days. So, he wrote ' Decorated pensioner's flat ' under the following competency categories : **Deadlines, Targets and Achieving; Attention to Detail, Teamwork**. That one experience can serve him for 3 competency examples.

John is 19. He has had one part-time job and one full-time job. When at school, he had a Saturday job washing cars. It did not involve meeting the customers but he did have to wash so many cars per hour and to a high standard. So, he writes Washed Cars under the competency category **Deadlines, Targets and Achieving** and also again under **Attention to Detail**. He had a full-time temporary job as a Mailroom Assistant in a team with an Insurance Company. So, he enters 'Mailroom Assistant ' under the **Teamwork** category. He remembers that the job involved carefully weighing the post and calculating the correct postage of envelopes and packages. So, he enters Mailroom Assistant Weighing under ' **Attention to Detail** '. He remembers that he had to liaise with the staff on all floors, taking their instructions and also receiving post from couriers . He enters 'Mailroom Liaison with staff and couriers' under the **Communication** competency. Since he had strict time deadlines each day to meet , he notes that under the **Deadlines, Targets and Achieving** competency.

Finally, since the job had its ups and downs in volumes of work due to mailshots , TV ads, etc, he had to be flexible over shifts, staying late and working overtime. He writes 'Required overtime at Mail job' under the **Change, Flexibility and Adaptability** category.

2.7   Do you get the idea ?

If John now applies for a job which has a competency interview and the interviewer asks him for examples of when he has ever had to pay attention to detail or work in a team or communicate with others or work to a deadline or be flexible at work, he has ready- made examples in his Experiences Autobiography. .

He has these examples because he has taken the time and trouble to think exactly and specifically of the actions he has done in the past, to write them down and then to assign them to one or more competencies. That is your challenge. The reward is a good job. Now do it !

2.8   If you are returning to work after a long time away from the workplace

If you are perhaps a parent or a carer who has been at home for some years and are now trying to get back into the world of work which is different from the equally demanding world of housework and caring, you will need to give employers examples of your behaviours which meet the required competencies.

Although returning to work can seem daunting, don't worry : millions have achieved it and so can you. Firstly, most employers are equally accepting of examples from outside the workplace. Secondly, you can easily build up a strong Experiences Autobiography with valid , excellent examples of your competence and skills by realising that what you have done in the home and with others are "transferable skills" . All you need is to get into the habit of closely identifying your actions.

For example, if you are asked in an interview for an example of how you have **organised**, you can state how you have organised your child's birthday party or playgroups or arranged babysitters or planned ahead for your child's new term. You have organised your time effectively so that all the washing, cleaning, ironing, shopping, school runs, visits to doctors and chemists and all meals are prepared on time and kids are bathed all on time. You know how much organising that takes so don't let others underestimate it.

If asked for an example of your **attention to detail,** you would tell of how you got all your kids to school on time each day, how you budgeted perfectly and how you paid all your bills perfectly without incurring any penalties. You budgeted ahead for birthdays, bills and emergencies too.

For examples of **flexibility and versatility**, you often had to adapt to unexpected circumstances, such as when your kids became ill, were sent home from school (teachers on strike, school snowed off,),your kids had accidents and you found a solution to the problem.

Communication skills ? You have had to deal with the teachers and PTA, the council, the DWP, HMRC for tax credits. You can mention the other groups you may be part of, including online forums.

Determination and resilience ? Describe how you stuck up for your child's rights through thick and thin in a prolonged struggle with the Education Department or school or how you won a long benefit claim for your child.

You will need to persuade prospective employers that the life skills you have developed over the years – and they are indeed valuable and considerable - are relevant to them and to the advertised job.

To do this, you will need to examine every single action you have taken while you have been out of the workplace. Yes, I know it is a laborious job but nothing comes easy to us in life and you will ultimately be rewarded if you do so. Write all your experiences into your **Experiences Autobiography**, as I have described.

2.9 If you are an ex-offender

Focus on the reskilling courses taken and say they were not easy to achieve with so many distractions. Focus on your determination to improve yourself and on your resilience. For Attention to Detail, you can tell of the precise measuring you had to do in your woodwork classes. For Teamwork, state how you were part of a team who met weekly to warn teenagers away from a life of crime involving knives or drugs or gangs or whatever. Many ex-offenders get jobs every day and so can you, if you persist.

2.9 If you are a young person with very little work experience

Don't despair. The same applies to you as to the members of the group in 2.8 You too can build up an Experiences Autobiography by relating all your school experiences and all the experiences with friends, on holidays, in various groups and in the community – even in online groups and friendships – as examples of your skills. You can even use experiences with your family members or friends. These are just as valid.

For example, when asked for examples of **Adapting to Change,** you can say how you adapted to a new home / teacher /6th form/ step-parent/ baby sibling/ the loss of someone or any sudden change, welcome or otherwise. Don't worry. The details I've given for each competency later in the book will help you describe how you did it. See 7.1

Attention to Detail – Any Maths, Science or Computing students should have no difficulty narrating how their equations or formulae had to be exact to balance or how their computer program they had coded had to be without a single error in order to run. Any Social Sciences students can state how they had to ensure their data was accurate. History students can say their dates had to perfect and Literature students can say their quotations had to be verbatim. See 7.2

For **Communication** examples, you can state how you had to carefully structure your essays : the need to plan them, to have a brief intro of a couple of sentences, a main body of two or three paragraphs where it develops and then a final paragraph where you summarise it all and perhaps state your conclusion. You might remember how you had to give a small speech or presentation to your class on your coursework or how you explained the internet or mobile phones or Skype to elderly people. See 7.3

For **Customer Service,** you might give examples from your Saturday job (include any training you were given for it) in a shop or on your uncle's market-stall / regular car-boot pitch or the times you helped to serve at your school fetes. Everyone has an uncle who has a market-stall or shop, where you gained valuable customer service experience. See 7.4

For examples of working to **Deadlines and Targets**, you might care to mention how you prioritised your assignments / essays/ coursework and exam preparation by deciding what was Urgent, what was Important and which was Non-urgent and allowing contingency Time for any emergencies. Note the specific examples and of how you organised things. Tell how you never failed to submit your work on time and never felt too rushed because you planned well. See 7.5

For **Decision Making**, stick with how you went about selecting your options or choosing your college or uni. State how you went about your decision. You'll find this in Chapter 7.6.

For **Drive, Determination and Resilience,** maybe you passed your exams after recovering from a bad accident or a family bereavement or divorce. Maybe you lost weight or eventually managed to run a half-marathon or ride 40 miles on your bike after several attempts. The point is that you persevered and didn't give up. Show them that. See 7.7

For **Teamworking** examples, you can narrate how you participated in a team project, perhaps how you contributed computer code or some ideas. Remember that you can use any experiences from outside of school, so tell of how you help the neighbourhood / community team clear up litter from the street / park / woods. Perhaps you played in a team, even an online one. That is valid too. See 8.8

A prospective employer is willing to accept all and any of your examples , if they are well prepared and you can show him that your past behaviour matches what he is looking for. Believe me, you can do it. Many have done it with my help and YOU can too. The Prime Minister , the President of the USA and the Pope had not done the job before but all had done something a bit similar. That's all you need.

The education system in Britain fails miserably to prepare school leavers for the world of work and it will come as a shock to most of you. What you must do is to get experience of some sort and volunteering is a good way. Don't mock it.

There are now many more types of opportunities, both indoors and outdoors. Even just two hours a morning will give you experience, a reference, new skills and more examples for your Experiences Autobiography. Moreover, you will make contacts and get to hear about job opportunities, not only from staff there but also from customers.

Charity shops are a really useful avenue for gaining experience of customer service, teamworking, attention to detail – probably the three most tested competencies. Don't look down on work in charity shops. I have seen lots of people develop from volunteers there to become managers and even district managers and not just in the retail sector. It is good experience. You will make new friends and new contacts. You will get to hear about jobs and upcoming jobs from the public.

When writing examples of your experiences, it doesn't matter that your work was unpaid : if you demonstrated great teamworking, you are a great teamworker whether the job was paid or voluntary. No one should be just "unemployed". You should be "unemployed and reskilling at college " or "unemployed and volunteering".

Before starting any voluntary work, ensure that you will be given a reference for satisfactory work and attendance after a reasonable time , usually 3 to 3 or 6 months.

Chapter 3   How to predict the competencies you might be asked

Okay, you've been called for an interview and you know or suspect that it will consist of competency questions. Your task now is to predict which competencies you will be tested on and to prepare your answers as best you can.

3.1   Deconstructing the job advert

How is it possible to predict the competencies ? There is , of course, no absolutely certain way of knowing in advance what you will be asked - but employers are very busy people, who don't waste their time. They will ask you about the competencies which are directly relevant to the job for which you are applying and these are contained in the job advert and in the job description. More information may be available on the company website about the competencies needed or in any application pack or supplementary guidance notes sent to you. The biggest clues will come from the job advert itself and it is by close analysis and deconstruction of the job advert that you will be able to predict the likely questions that the interviewers will ask.

Let us examine a real job advert :

Example A

Customer Service Adviser , South East London, £ 8.50 per hour

As a Customer Service Advisor you will be responsible for the first line and follow up customer contacts by dealing with a mixture of inbound and outbound contacts, taking calls, writing letters and emails and assisting in projects to continuously improve our customer services.

Duties include: Respond to customer enquiries in warm, friendly and personable tone ---- Deal with customer complaints ---Log calls on to the PC ----Provide customers with product and service information-----Report and escalate any priority issues ----Recognise and use opportunities to promote other services-----Administration : Write clear, concise and customer focused letters and emails.

Skills and Knowledge:Excellent written and verbal communications skills are essential---Must have previous work experience within a customer services environment -----Experience of multi-tasking (simultaneously using the telephone and PC based applications) preferred

The idea now is to carefully scrutinize the advert and to identify which competencies the interviewer is demanding. Read the advert carefully a few times. Try to get a feel for the job. What will the worker be doing all day long ?

Having read the job advert, do you think the interviewer will ask us about Project Management skills ? Absolutely not. It is not that kind of job and there is no mention of that. Leadership skills ? Again, highly unlikely because nothing is mentioned in the advert about leadership. We must focus on which skills are being sought or implied.

We need to write down the required competencies. The title of the job is sometimes a real help and in this case, it is a real giveaway. So, taking a new sheet of paper, we write **Customer Service**. Next, it says ' *Dealing with inbound contacts* ' and '*Writing letters and emails* ', so we write down ' **Communication** '.
'*Respond to customer enquiries*' and '*Deal with customer complaints* ' is already is covered by Customer Service. It says ' *Log calls on to the PC'*, so we write **Attention to Detail** . We see '*Recognise and see opportunities to promote other services*' and so write **Negotiation and Persuasion** . Administration ? We have already covered this in Communication.

It says that written and communication skills are '**essential**'. This is a **major clue** in predicting what questions will be asked in a competency interview. Whenever the job advert or any job description states the word '**essential**' or it says ' **must have**', then it is almost guaranteed that you will be asked to give an example of that.

Here, it also says 'must have' previous experience in a customer services environment. It asks for multi-tasking, so we write Change. Flexibility, Adaptability .

3.2   Prioritizing the competencies

We have noted five competencies but we must now prioritize them. We look to see which of those were demanded as ' **essential** ' or '**must have** ' qualities. They were Communication Skills and Customer Service Skills. It is a certainty that these will be asked at the interview and a high probability that the other three will be the other questions at the interview. On average, interviewers ask three or four competency questions. In later chapters we look at the potential questions in greater detail and how to answer them.

Occasionally, employers will also use words such as imperative, vital, key , paramount, critical or crucial. If any of these appear, treat them   as **essential** competencies and expect to be asked about them at the interview.

Let us examine now another job advert :

Example B

Meter Reader South West London 37 hours per week - flexible working between 8am-8 pm   Weekly Pay £281 plus up to £100 bonus and additional mileage allowance

The role :   Working with XXXX, you will represent many of the UK's leading energy providers, visiting a wide variety of customers at their homes.

•   You will work within 30 mile radius of your home address and mileage is fully expensed from the moment you leave your house.

•   Visiting people at their homes you will be reading their gas and electricity meters, completing visual safety checks and accurately recording your readings onto a handheld terminal

•   The ability to plan your own route and manage your diary and workload to achieve the targets set for that day/week is essential

Must have had some previous customer service experience. If you are self motivated and would be committed to this long term opportunity and a resident of the SW postcode, please apply by sending your CV to YYY.

Read it carefully. From the first bullet point, we might guess that **Customer Service** might be asked. The second bullet point gives us no clues. The third definitely confirms our suspicions about experience of Customer Service and also the necessity for experience of **Attention to Detail**. The final bullet point tells us that the competencies of **Time Management and Targets** achieving will be required. The last paragraph tells us that   Customer Service is demanded, as is self-motivation, so we note **Self-Motivation** too.

What do you do now ? You prioritize by going back and looking for those all important words .. .... ' **essential** ' and '**must have.**'

The employer used 'essential ' in the fourth bullet point, so we can expect the employer to focus on the candidate's diary management skills and his ability to achieve his targets. Customer service was 'essential', so the candidate must prepare good examples of when he has provided excellent customer service. Attention to detail and motivation seem less mportant to the employer.

Example C

> *Role: Prisoner Custody Officer Hours: 40 during training and then 35 hours per week when fully trained*
>
> *We currently require Prison Custody Officers working 35 hours per week on various shifts. Your role as a Prisoner Custody Officer is to provide a safe and secure environment for people committed into custody by the courts. A Prisoner Custody Officer supervises and manages prisoners, promotes good behaviour, ensures that all rules, orders and instructions are followed to ensure those in our care are treated with dignity and respect whilst maintaining safety and security.   Previous experience is not essential as full training will be provided. To secure one of these demanding but rewarding roles you will need to be able to demonstrate first class communication skills, the ability to write concise but accurate and clear reports, be committed to team work and have the awareness to ensure security is maintained at all times.*
>
> *MAIN DUTIES:*
> *Ensure the security and welfare of those in our care is maintained at all times.*
> *Ensure all incidents are reported and dealt with effectively, including assaults, substance misuse and self harm*
> *Uphold respect for Prisoners, their property, rights and dignity*
> *Essential Skills and Experience:*
> *Ability to work as part of a team*
> *Ability to report accurately both verbally and in writing*
> *Excellent communication skills*

Read the above job advert carefully and list the competencies that the employer would most likely demand. The ad says that previous experience of maintaining safety and security is **not** essential. What **is** essential and what I hope you have noted are the following :

Teamwork , **Communication** skills and **Customer Service** Skills. Although 'Customer Service ' has not been explicitly stated, you would be dealing with other people and so this is implied and to be expected. The ability to write clear, concise and accurate reports is demanded. Also, in the first paragraph, did you notice that it says : A Prison Custody Officer .. *'promotes good behaviour'* ? This to me indicates that they are looking for someone who has good negotiating skills. Someone who can persuade disruptive or upset prisoners to calm down . It is reinforced by the last line in Essential Skills... *'The ability to handle stressful situations '* That, of course is advanced interpersonal behaviour, which comes under good Communication Skills but also under Negotiation and Persuasion. People with high Negotiation and Persuasion skills can quickly get themselves out of stressful situations.

I would suggest that ' promotes good behaviour' might easily have been missed if you had read the advert in a perfunctory manner. It is imperative that you **analyse job descriptions very carefully**, word by word and read between the lines.

Ask yourself :Which four or five competencies, **according to this advert**, am I **most** likely to be asked ? Then ask, which are the most likely **two or three** ?

3.3 Summary   You should now understand how to analyse job adverts to predict which competencies are required.

- Read the advert several times.
- Read it word for word.
- Remember to read any other job-description or material that came in the job-pack and anything on the company website which may give clues.
- Sometimes competencies are explicitly stated, sometimes not.

Prioritize those marked as **essential**, or ' **must have** ' or similarly described. You **will** be questioned on them.

Chapter 4 How to predict the interview questions

4.1 Predicting the questions

Although it is not possible to predict all the questions you might be asked, it is possible to predict a good deal of them. If you have narrowed down the required competencies, as outlined in the previous chapter, you are homing in on the action. No two jobs are exactly alike and no two companies are exactly alike so it is impossible to be cetain. Once again, we must return to the actual job advert and give it a close reading. Let us return to Example A from Chapter 3 again. We decided that **Customer Service** and **Communication** were the two most important competencies demanded.

4.2   The most frequently asked questions on **Customer Service** are : Tell me of a time when you have :

1.   Given great customer service / Gone the extra mile for a customer.
2.   Dealt with a difficult customer / Handled a complaint.
3.   Failed to deal with an awkward customer.

Examining the advert, we see that we are expected to respond to enquiries in a friendly manner and provide product information. So, we can predict that we shall be asked question 1…. given good customer service. You will need to look through your Experiences Autobiography for an example of such an occasion.

Since the ad clearly says you will be handling complaints, we can predict that you could be asked question 2 …handled a complaint. You will need an example of when you have done this.

Interviewers often ask Q3. My advice is to never say anything negative about yourself in an interview. Ever. If asked this question, reply that there are no " difficult" customers but some are a little more "demanding " than others and you see that as a challenge and an opportunity to use more of your people skills. Say that you have **never** failed to deal with a customer to their satisfaction. Never say anything negative about yourself . Ever. Either in an interview situation or even when you talk to yourself every day, as we all do. If asked question 3, give an example of how you successfully handled a demanding customer.

At this point it is necessary to point out that the wording of a question can vary greatly. The same question can be asked in many different ways and you must be very awake and sharp in an interview situation to realise this. I'll say more about this later.

4.3   The competency ' **Communication** ' can generate many questions, depending on the job. Naturally, there is a great overlap between Communication skills and Customer Service skills. These are all interpersonal skills.

The most frequently asked questions by interviewers on **Communication** are "Give me an example of when you :
1.   Communicated something difficult to someone. / Presented something clearly.
2.   Adapted your communication style to suit the listener / audience.
3.   Had to communicate something with sensitivity and tact."

From the advert, it's fair to expect Q1 to be asked, because we are, after all, trying for a job in a call centre ! Next, since the advert states that you would be writing 'customer-focused letters ', I would very much expect Q2 to be asked.

Next, we concluded that the competencies of Attention to Detail *and* Negotiation / Persuasion would arise. So, a question such as *"Give me an example of when you have had to work with great accuracy "* or *"Tell me of a time when you had to work with great attention to detail "* can be expected for this job. You will need really good examples of meticulous work to high standards. If you have had a financial background or even counted money on a till, you will need to show that you worked to zero tolerance of errors. You prided yourself on your till always being penny-perfect when you handed over to your colleague. This might have only been a Saturday job long ago.

4.4   Similarly, since the advert stated that you must "promote services", you could easily be asked one of the most common questions of the **Negotiation - Persuasion** competency category Tell me about a time when you :

1.   Successfully negotiated something.
2.   Motivated someone to do something and how you overcame their objections.
3.   Argued your case for something and how you won it.
4.   Persuaded someone to buy something or do something.

I would expect Q 1 to be the most appropriate for this job.

It's always possible in a job such as this that the interviewer will ask a question about the candidate's ability to fit into a team . Unusually for a call-centre, teamwork has not been mentioned in the advert, Perhaps this call-centre is not open-plan and each worker is quite self-contained in his own pod for most of the day and has little interaction with colleagues. Nevertheless, I would always have an example of teamwork ready for the interview , such as one in response to "Give me an example of when you have worked well in / contributed well to a team "

The ability to multi-task was "preferred" but not essential. It could come up as a question. It is best to be prepared for it with an example of when you have done more than one job at once with no loss of quality. Mothers are experts at this.

To summarise then, the most likely questions that will asked for Example A are:

(a) Tell me a time when you have given great customer service / gone the extra mile for the customer . (b) Tell me time when you have handled a difficult customer who had a complaint. (c) Give an example of when you have had to explain something difficult to someone in a clear manner. (d) Tell me of when you have had to communicate your style to suit the customer. (e) Give me an example of when you persuaded someone to buy something.

4.5 Example B from Chap 3.

Re-read Example B from Chap 3 and our concluded competencies from the previous chapter. The most common questions asked around **Deadlines / Targets / Achieving** are :

Give me an example of when you :
1. Successfully met your targets within challenging deadlines.
2. Failed to meet your targets. / Missed a deadline.
3. Your greatest achievement.

Again, the wording used can differ slightly. It's clear that this is a very target-driven job, where the bonus is almost 25% of the basic wage. It is certain that one of the questions will be similar to Q 1. The employer will want to hear an example of when the candidate has had to work to demanding targets and deadlines and how he achieved them. He could also very well ask Q2, since this is also very popular with interviewers. The candidate should never portray himself in a negative light. Ever. If he was ever in danger of missing a target or deadline, he can relate how he renegotiated the deadline or enlisted help from a colleague to achieve his target or that he never missed deadlines because he always had the foresight to have a contingency plan inbuilt into his schedule. You never miss deadlines. Do you understand ? You never ever say anything negative about yourself in an interview. Ever. Ever. Do you understand ? No exceptions. Ever.

Since he is entering customers' homes, he could well be asked one of the common **Customer Service** favourites :

Tell me of a time when you have :

1. Given great customer service or gone the extra mile for a customer.
2. Dealt with a difficult customer or handled a complaint.
3. Failed to deal with an awkward customer.

In this job, he will be reading the gas and electricity meters of people so that they can receive bills for their usage. Nobody likes receiving bills , so he can expect a cool welcome. Occasionally he may even experience hostility. He is quite likely to be asked any of the above . If asked Q2 or Q3, he replies that there are no " difficult" customers but some are a little more demanding than others and he sees that as a challenge and an opportunity to use more of his people skills.. He has **never** failed to deal with a customer to their satisfaction. I would expect Q2 because the employer will know that the applicant will regularly have to deal will uncooperative customers and will want to know how he has dealt with that in the past.

We concluded that he would be asked about **Attention to detail** , so we would expect a question such as *"Give me an example of when you have had to work to great accuracy "* or *"Tell me of a time when you had to work with great attention to detail ".*

4.6 Finally, we noted that **Self-Motivation** was called for and so it is likely that the employer will ask him for an example of when he has motivated himself . The most common questions are :

Give me an example of when you :

1. Have shown real drive and determination to succeed.

2. Have motivated yourself .

3. Recovered from a serious setback.

Here, since the applicant will be faced with customers being out when he calls and the need to nevertheless achieve daily targets, it will require constant motivation and drive and the likelihood is that he will be asked Q1 or possibly Q2 and he will need good examples of how he has kept himself motivated in frustrating circumstances.

Summary :

(a) Give me an example of when you successfully met your targets within challenging deadlines. (b) Tell me of a time when you failed to meet your target. (c) Tell me of a time when you dealt with a difficult customer. (d) Give me an example of when you have had to work with great attention to detail. e) Give me an example of when you have shown real drive or determination to succeed.

4.7 Example C from Chap 3.

Re-read Example C from Chapter 3 carefully and the concluded competencies. The most frequently asked questions on **Teamwork** are :

Give me an example of when you :

1. Worked well in a team. / Helped a team achieve its target.
2. Had a problem with a team colleague.
3. Resolved conflict within a team.

It is certain that the candidate would be asked **Q1,**" Worked within a team" and perhaps Q2 also but I would not rate this as a high probability.

The most frequently asked questions on **Communication** are :

Give me an example of when you :

1. Communicated something difficult to someone. / Presented something clearly.
2. Adapted your communication style to suit the listener / audience.
3. Had to communicate something with sensitivity and tact.

For this particular post, it clearly states that the candidate will need to report clearly and accurately both verbally and in writing. Therefore **Q 1** will certainly be asked. He will be asked for an example of when he has either had to report in person to someone , relaying clear and exact messages or else when he has written reports. It is highly likely that Q3 could be asked , since this is a role which requires great tact. I would say that there is a possibility, though a lesser one, that Q2 will be asked.

The most frequently asked questions by interviewers on **Customer Service** are : Tell me of a time when you have :

1. Given great customer service or gone the extra mile for a customer.
2. Dealt with a difficult customer or handled a complaint.
3. Failed to deal with an awkward customer.

Any of these questions could be asked, since it is a customer-facing role. I would suggest that **Q2** is almost certain to be asked : " Dealt with a difficult customer " and possibly Q3 too because nobody like paying bills. . I think Q1 is less likely to be asked because the role of a Prison Officer is not to ensure that a prisoner will "Have a nice day ".

The most frequently asked questions on **Negotiation and Persuasion** are : Tell me about a time when you :

1. Successfully negotiated something.

2. Motivated someone to do something and how you overcame their objections.

3. Argued your case for something and how you won it.

4. Persuaded someone to buy something or do something.

In a job such as this, the Prison Officers will always be faced with objections and I think Q 2 is quite possible. Q1 is possible too. Since prisoners have little bargaining power, I would not expect Q 1 to arise.

Summary of likely questions :

(a) Give me an example of when you have worked well in a team.(b) Give me an example of when you have had to communicate / report something clearly and accurately. (c) Tell me about a time when you have had to communicate something with sensitivity and tact. (d) Tell me a time when you have dealt with a difficult customer. (e) Give me an example of when you have motivated someone to do something and how you overcame their objections. (f) Tell me about a time when you have persuaded someone to do something.

Chapter 5 How to answer competency questions

So, you have been through the advert with a fine toothcomb and concluded which competencies are required. Then, you very carefully analysed it again and have predicted some of the likely questions. Your next step is to look through your Experiences Autobiography and find experiences which can be used as examples for your answers.

5.1   Using an experience creatively

It's important to realize that an experience can be used to answer several competencies. Remember Josh (Chap. 2.2) who sent the urgent fax ? He could use that experience to answer both a Problem-Solving question which was thrown at him or an Initiative question. If someone had worked on a helpdesk in a supermarket, answering customer enquiries, they could use that experience for any Customer Service, Problem-Solving, Communication or Teamwork question. If you had worked shifts on a till in a shop, you could use that as an example for Attention to Detail or Flexibility or Communication or Customer Service. If you had taken on that job after suffering a major setback in your life such as a bereavement or separation or illness, then you also use it for Drive or Determination or / Resilience or Self Motivation.. Be careful about using illness however, unless it was just an accident, as employers generally do not like to hear about illness.

5.2   Choosing your examples

Always try to choose an example which matches the job description as closely as possible. For example , there is a job as a cashier in a super-market. The advert demands that you have a great attention to detail. You have three examples of this. Firstly, you worked in a post room , weighing letters. Secondly you worked as a cashier in a betting-shop. Thirdly, you measured and cuts lots of material for your hobby of home-decorating.

It is best to use the example of your time as a cashier because this most closely resembles this job for which you are now applying. **Always try to** choose an example which matches the job description and the job grade, as closely as possible.

5.3 The question format

The interviewer will most often use one of the following phrases :

- "Give me an example of when you ...."
- "Tell me about a time when you ...."
- "Describe a situation in which you ...."
- "What has been your greatest / worst ....?"
- "Have you ever ....?   When did you ...... ?"

5.4 The **C.A.R.** answer format

The simplest way to answer the interviewer's questions is to use the **C.A.R format** to tell a small story, which will last around three minutes on average. Using this small , simple format ensures that your story has a logical flow.

Firstly, you will set the scene by describing the **CIRCUMSTANCE** . This is telling the interviewer what the situation or problem was that needed your attention. It is putting things in context.

Next, you will describe what **ACTION** you took to remedy the problem. This is where you go into the specifics and spell out exactly what you did and it gives you the opportunity to sell yourself to the employer. This is where you demonstrate how you have the competency which is being sought in the job advert. You tell **how you have already successfully dealt** with this situation in the past. You must detail not only what action you took but what skills you employed. Wherever possible, try to choose an example which is similar to the job you are now applying for. Wherever possible, try to demonstrate that you have **already done** exactly what the interviewer is asking.

Finally, you summarise the **RESULT**, detailing the benefits to your past employer and team and if possible, with hard figures if you improved productivity or saved money. If you can't quantify the experience with figures, describe what you learned from it. Also, add any praise or awards you received.

Approximately 10 % of your time should be spent setting the scene, 75% describing the action that you took and 15% describing the result.

5.5 Writing your scripts

You have identified experiences which you can use for your examples. Hopefully, you will have several for each competency. Don't panic if you have only one or none at this moment. Choose the strongest and most relevant example you have.

The next step is that you will write a script for yourself for each example, practise it and then use it at the interview.

When writing your script, you will need to consider the following : **C.A.R**

Circumstance : What was the situation ? What was the task you faced ? What was the problem that needed solving ? How did you get to be given it ?

Action : What action did you take and why ? Were there several approaches you could have adopted ? If so, why did you elect to take the one you did ? What skills did you use which demonstrate the competency exactly ? Show the steps you took and any difficulties you faced. How did you overcome them ? If people resisted you, how did you counter their objections ? Include key indicator words which demonstrate the competency. These are provided for the most common competencies in Chapters 7 and 8.

Result : State how you completed the task and what you learned from it. State the benefits to the employer or the team or the customer. If you have improved productivity or saved money, **quantify it with hard figures** . Don't say " I made my company a lot of money. ". Instead, say " I increased turnover by 5%, which equated to £20,000 per year." Or, " I saved my employer 7% on his stationery charges, which equated to £800 per year". Then maybe quote any praise or positive feedback you received from a customer or your Team Leader or any bonus or rewards.

5.6   You are expected to boast !

In our normal life, we are taught not to boast . It is frowned upon and we isolate people who do. However, there is one exception in life when boasting is not only acceptable but expected and that is in an interview. You must absolutely tell the interviewer how capable you are because you only have this one opportunity. He is not a mind reader and can't know your abilities. You must spell them out for him. Be proud of your skills and your achievements. You are allowed to boast in an interview but boast about your skills and achievements, not about YOU.

Say that you are proud of having achieved XYZ , not because you are brilliant but because you worked extremely hard or you made many sacrifices or overcame many obstacles to get it. I want you right now to change your mindset about any reservation or shyness you have about boasting. Believe me - it is expected in an interview. Don't let that precious opportunity pass you by. It might not come again. The employer wants to hear your examples.!!

Example 1 "Give me an example of when you have been adaptable to change "

Now for an example. Mark has read a job advert. It states twice that he must be adaptable to change and so he is expecting to be asked for an example of this. He looks through his Experiences Autobiography and he finds an example of when he worked for local government (the council) in the public transport section and when he was suddenly told that he would have to work in the Information Unit the following week to cover sickness absence. He had only ever been shown around there once before and knew that there was IT and switchboard, which was unfamiliar to him .

He knew none of the staff and knew that the place was manically busy. His usual job was giving out info to the public face-to-face but he was suddenly going to have to adapt to working in a very busy call-centre environment, something he had never done before. The challenge for Mark now is to script this in a way that he will be able to demonstrate his competency in the best way. He will write his script, change it a few times until he is happy with it and read it to friends and family to get their feedback. Maybe he will record himself on tape or into his computer or phone to hear how he comes across and to time himself. He will practise, practise, practise.

I worked in local government in the Transport Department. Normally, my job was working in the shop selling all sorts of transport tickets to the public and answering their enquiries on the routes of buses, trains, ferries and the underground . But one Thursday, my Team Leader told me that the following week, I would be needed in the Information Unit because several staff there had gone down with a virus.

It was a call-centre environment there and they worked on a very large switchboard that I was unfamiliar with and they had other IT and telephony that I hadn't used before too.

So, the first thing I did was I adopted a positive approach to the change, seeing it as an opportunity to learn more skills and more efficient working practices and maybe add something to my CV. The second thing I did was to start to manage the change instead of becoming a victim of it by planning a visit. I asked my Team Leader if I could spend some time the next day, the Friday, at the Information Unit, familiarising myself with the equipment and acquainting myself with the staff and the layout of everything. She agreed to let me spend the Friday there.

So, I learned as much as I could before the big change. I'm really glad I made that plan because there was lots to learn. They liaised with many external partners such as the Police, Coastguard, Emergency Services, the Press, the utility companies etc. and I learned how to do that. I familiarised myself with as much of the tech as I possibly could and even the canteen, toilets and my own route there, so as minimize the strangeness the following week.

The result was that on the Monday morning, I hit the ground running. Those two weeks were extremely pressurised but because I had planned the change and managed it, it had been a disruption to me but not an upheaval. I had learned new switchboard skills , which I added to my CV. The Team Leader of the Information Unit was so impressed with my work after that fortnight, that he asked me to join his team permanently. I had decided to be the manager of the change, not its victim .

Notice that that he used **some** of the all-important **competency indicators of Change** ... *adopted a positive approach..... saw it as an opportunity to learn more skills ... planned the change... made full use of new tech .... managed the change*

From Chapter 7 onwards, you can see that I have listed key indicators of the Adapting to Change competency. He used some words which all demonstrate that he was adaptable and flexible to the process of change. He managed and planned his two week disruption in advance, rather than reacting to it.

When you compose any script, you will be aiming to include some key indicators of the competency in it.

Notice that Mark explained the background to the story. He explained how things were before the change.

Notice how he has spent *most of his script describing the action that he took* : He adopted a positive approach.... He embraced the change instead of resisting it. You must always include that in your answer. He managed the change.... He asked his Team Leader ...He familiarised himself with as much as he could in advance .

Notice that he used   " *I* " throughout the narrative.

Notice that he explained what he had learned and how he had benefited from the experience. He ended the story powerfully, both in saying that the Unit's Team Leader tried to headhunt him and also by repeating a memorable slogan ... manager of the change, not the victim.

5.7 Using effective, descriptive action words

When writing your scripts, it is important to use specific, descriptive **action words** which tell the employer exactly what you did. It is not enough to keep saying " I did this and then I did that and then I did something else." Did is useless.

If you are giving an example of ' Attention to Detail ', it sounds far better to say " I carefully **monitored** the dials" rather than " I checked the dials." If you were answering an ' Initiative ' question, it's better to say that you **"pre-empted** a potentially serious accident in the workplace " rather than you stopped someone slipping on water. When giving an example of ' Problem Solving' and telling how , while resolving the problem, you noticed part of the procedure was no longer necessary so you **streamlined** it. That sounds much better than " I cut parts out ". Employers like to hear " streamlined", since it suggests a saving of their money. You will find a list of action words to use in Chapter 9. Add your own words to the list as you go along but a word of warning : make sure you know the correct meaning of a word before using it. Use the words for accuracy, not for ego.

5.8 Keep your script

When you are happy with your script, having perhaps have tried it out in front of family or friends, put it in your Experiences Autobiography. Hopefully, it will help you to land this job and then you will not need again for a long time but do keep it, to save you having to write it again.

5.9 Teamwork example

This time, here is an example in which the interviewer is asking about Teamwork **Example 2 " _Tell me about a time when you have worked well in a team_ "**

Answer : When the council was selling off our estate to a Housing Association, it invited the tenants to form a tenants' association. I became a member of the 20 person team. There were many issues to be discussed - such as whether the high-rise blocks were to be demolished or not and there were different groups of people with different agendas and fears. The team itself was quite diverse so it was going to be a real challenge to get everyone to work together.

I promoted equality and diversity by ensuring that the pensioners and teenagers got just as much speaking time as everyone else. Over the course of the six months, I respected and valued the diverse views, perspectives and experience of all the other members. I always gave gentle and positive feedback to the suggestions from others and similarly, I respected and accepted the feedback from them. I acted as one of the main liaison points between the team and all external interested parties , such as the Police, Social Services, Probation, etc.

I contributed to the team with my ideas and knowledge and I contributed to the team morale with humour and enthusiasm. I resolved disputes and conflict among team-members by finding common ground and showing that contradictory views are often misunderstandings or misinformation. I treated everyone with respect at all times. I compromised over decisions and put the common group goal above my own.

The result was that the estate was transferred over to the Housing Association and I facilitated in playing a part in ensuring that everyone had had a say in the process. I had helped several diverse groups to work together as a team. I had gained valuable experience from liaison with several agencies , which later stood me in good stead as the references got me a good job.

Notice that he set the scene and explained that there were diverse people with different agendas

Notice that the bulk of the script is taken up with the Action that he took … I promoted…I respected…I gave ….I acted….I contributed………I resolved……etc.

Notice that he included **some competency indicators of Teamwork** : *fostered inclusion by promoting equality and diversity… respected diverse views, perspectives and experience… gave gentle, positive feedback… respected and accepted feedback…. contributed my ideas… resolved disputes … shared my ideas and knowledge … treated everyone with respect … contributed to the team morale with humour or enthusiasm … compromised … helped*

These are all words which tell the interviewer that he is an excellent team-worker. It could also be used as an example of Diversity.

5.10 Checking your script   You will not get your script right the first time and will have to amend it several times before you are happy with it.

- Is most of it taken up by the action part of what you actually did ?

- Have you included everything ?

- Have you repeated yourself by accident ?

- Have you mostly spoken about what **you** did ?

- Have you chosen an example which is similar to the job you are now applying for ?

- Have you described the benefits to you or the team or company or customer and if appropriate, been able to **quantify** them with hard figures and percentages ?

- Have you said what you learned and/ how you have grown from the experience ?

- Have you **finished with a strong impact** , that the employer will remember ?

5.11   Match your example to the job

When you look through your Autobiography, it is important to always use an experience which matches the duties and grade of the job you are now applying for, as closely as possible. For example, let us imagine that you are told to give an example of a time you have delivered great customer service. If you have 7 or 8 examples of when you have given great customer service and the job you are now going for is in a call-centre requiring some sales or persuasion, look for which one your examples where you have given great customer service whilst also persuading someone. Similarly, if the job description mentions a requirement for problem-solving, use one of your customer service examples where you also solved a problem for the customer. In other words, don't just select any old example from your lists. Carefully select which of your experiences is best suited to the job and grade you are now applying for. The more examples you build up, the easier this becomes.

5.12   If you can't think of any examples

If you have really spent time looking back at all the experiences in your life, both in work and outside, as I have described in chapter 2 and you have looked at the examples given under the competencies in chapters 7 and 8 and you still can't think of any examples of things you have done which match the competencies in the job advert, then I would suggest that the job may not be right for you. Listen to your heart. It is the best guide. Unless you are reaching out for a radically different change of career, it seems that you could well be going for a job that might be unsuitable for you. Are you sure you want to do this ? You can never be happy unless you are true to yourself. Follow your own inner nature, no matter what. In work, there are too many square pegs in round holes. You will never be happy in life until you find the right hole for yourself.

5.13 If you can't memorise your scripts

Practise your scripts after you have decided on the final draft and are happy with it. Then practise again and again. Some people have used a tape-recorder or mobile-phone to record themselves then play it back again and again until they know it off by heart, like a pop song. However, if you feel that your script is fine for an application form but that you have the memory of a goldfish and are unable to remember the whole script, you can either write a much shorter script or else **just note down key points**. Pick the bones out of them. In either case, it is vital that you stay with the C.A.R format and also that you mention a few key indicators of the competency.

Chapter 6 : What to do and what NOT to do

THINGS YOU MUST DO :

✓ Try to choose an example which matches the duties and the grade in the job description as much as possible

✓ Use examples from any area of your life.

✓ Have more than one example prepared for each competency

✓ Talk in specifics about what you did, relating your skills to the competency and to **THIS** job, if possible.

✓ Talk about what **YOU** did, not what the team did.

✓ Detail **HOW** you achieved it.

✓ Don't spend too much time setting the scene ... around 10%

✓ Convey as much information in the shortest possible time, emphasising key skills.

✓ **Quantify** your success, if appropriate, with figures and stats. If not, say you were praised by someone.

✓ Boast about your skills, not about you. Say your achievements are due to hard work and sacrifice, just as much as your skills.

✓ Stay focused on the question.

✓ Ensure your example has a happy ending !

✓ Finish with a **strong impact** and with you being praised, if that's appropriate.

✓ Practice your scripts in front of friends or family , if possible.

Things you must <u>NOT</u> do :

x   **Don't assume** the employer knows the background. Set the context.

x   **Don't generalise** : eg Don't say "I'm always.....(polite to customers)". The employer is not interested in how you normally are. He wants an example of what you have DONE <u>already</u> which shows a skill.

x   **Don't give a job description** : eg Don't say "My job involves" ..or " I do this .." The employer is not interested in what your job involves. He wants an example of what you've DONE.

x   **Don't theorize** : eg Don't say "Well, I would / I generally. / I tend to ." The employer is not interested in what you <u>would</u> do. He wants an example of what you HAVE DONE in the past which demonstrates the competency.

x   **Don't assert** : eg Don't say " It is very important to".... (get along with your colleagues).. The employer is not interested in your assertions. He wants to hear an example of something you have DONE, which shows that ability.

x   **Don't depersonalise it** : eg Don't say " <u>We</u> decided to ..." Say what **YOU** did, not what others did . Use " **I** ", not " We ".

x   **Don't use jargon**, abbreviations or slang. Don't assume the employer will understand your private language. Don't blind him with science.

x   **Don't be unbalanced.** Spend most of the time on the **ACTION** part

x   **Don't malign anyone.** Don't criticize customers, past or current employers, bosses or colleagues.

x   **Don't use controversial subjects as examples.** Stay with safe topics.

x   **Don't try to come across as Superman** : the examples don't have to be extraordinary. Just come across as being very good at your job.

x   **Don't talk for too long !** Be concise and crisp. Don't beat about the bush or waffle.

Chapter 7

7.1 The Adapting to Change Competencies

The interviewer wants to know how you have coped with sudden change . You must demonstrate that you had a POSITIVE ATTITUDE towards it and that you adapted to new working methods. You must show that you EMBRACE change, seeing it as a great OPPORTUNITY - to learn new skills and new good working practices, make new friends, improve your CV, and to grow as a person - and not something to be feared. You must show that you were ENTHUSIASTIC about the change and how it benefitted you and the organisation in some way. You must show that you keep up to date with change, especially new technology, so that new changes are not so new or frightening. You must show that you don't collapse or freak out in times of uncertainty or ambiguity.

None of us like constant change . We find it disruptive and I have yet to meet a colleague who likes the capitalist American nonsense of hot-desking (having no desk of your own but having to run round and find an empty one and log into a PC) or multi-tasking (having to do four or five jobs simultaneously) but in your example, you must appear to be flexible, open-minded and enthusiastic about new ideas.

- I took a positive "can do " approach to change, seeing it as an opportunity to learn skills and strengthen my CV
- I was flexible, enthusiastic and open to new ideas
- I was willing to adapt to develop new skills
- I supported and made full use of new technology
- I kept myself up-to-date with new technology
- I kept calm and didn't panic in changing circumstances
- I adapted my routine when there was sudden change
- I adjusted positively to rapidly changing priorities and simultaneous demands.
- I adapted my behaviour when working practices changed
- I adapted my work to cope when priorities changed
- I learned from my experiences and those of others and I adjusted accordingly

- I changed my behaviour as a result of feedback
- I multi-tasked, playing several different roles
- I revised my plans, decisions and working methods in the light of new information
- I was flexible when faced with unexpected obstacles and delays
- I worked effectively in situations of ambiguity and uncertainty
- I always managed the change, rather than becoming a victim of it

Here are some examples. You should have similar ones in your Experiences Autobiography. In an interview, ensure you include the competencies stated in 7.1

7.1 ex   20 Adapting to Change Examples :

1. You adapted to a new boss or teacher or colleague.
2. You transferred to a new site or shop or location.
3. You were asked to take on new tasks and responsibilities. You took them on with enthusiasm.
4. You learned new software or technology or equipment.
5. You retrained or went on a course.
6. You had your shift pattern suddenly altered.
7. You were suddenly caught up in an unexpected fire, disturbance or crisis. You coped with calmness and positivity.
8. You lost your job but adapted.
9. You had to go part-time or job-share. You adapted by finding another part-time job.
10. You had to move home and settle into a new environment
11. You reacted appropriately to an unexpected situation
12. You raised kids. That certainly involved adapting to sudden changes !
13. You volunteered to change shifts or holidays to help someone out
14. You adapted to new technology at home - a new type of phone/computer/ modem or to a new software system at work

Example 15 : Two staff suddenly left in one week. So, you readjusted your shifts and also volunteered to do extra hours until a new worker started. Emphasise that you worked smarter rather than that you simply did extra hours.

Example 16 : You worked in the storeroom of a shoe shop and were told that in two weeks' time, you would have to work on the till. You adopted a positive approach and asked if you could spend 10 minutes of your lunch observing the till cashiers at work, since you knew nothing about debit cards, etc. That was agreed. When you began your till training, it was so much easier.

"Tell me of a time when you have been adaptable to sudden change" Example 17 :

When I worked as a secretary, I had arranged the monthly meeting at the office for the managers in our area. That morning when I arrived in work, I found that there was rain coming in through the roof of the conference room. This was only about three hours before the meeting was due to start.

So, I adopted a positive approach and stayed calm. I checked to see if any other rooms could possibly be used but none could. I then quickly phoned each manager's secretary and told them not to let their manager set off until I had found a new location.

Since my manager was off, I took the initiative. I adjusted to the rapidly changing situation by researching local hotels and chose one which was highly recommended by a variety of sources for its high standards of service. I phoned it and booked a room there. I also booked some refreshments. I took the opportunity to have them send details of their services. I then contacted the secretaries again with the precise details of the new location and arranged for the meeting to begin a little later in order to allow everyone sufficient time to arrive.

The result was that the meeting went ahead successfully. Since midweek rates were very cheap and he could network, the regional manager was very impressed and decided to hold all future meetings there.

Notice how some competency **indicators of Adapting to Change** were included : ...*adopted a positive approach* .... *stayed calm*......*adjusted to the rapidly changing situation by* .....

Example 18 : You planned a church fete. That day, there were rain and gales forecast, so rather than cancelling it, you improvised and moved it into the church hall.

Example 19 : You planned your child's birthday party in the garden but when the weather suddenly turned bad, you adapted by moving it indoors.

Example 20 : You were doing one job and were suddenly asked to do another job. So, you delegated some of your work or asked a colleague to take some of your tasks in return for a future favour.

7.2 The Attention to Detail Competencies

The interviewer wants to be sure that you have a keen eye for detail; that you paid great attention to your work ; that you controlled your errors.

- I double-checked the accuracy of my work using a structured checklist
- I had someone else check my work, if appropriate
- I measured everything at least twice. " Measure twice, cut once."
- I was careful, meticulous and thorough
- I continually sought to improve my accuracy
- I took pride in my work
- I had a zero tolerance policy to my own mistakes
- I prevented distractions to my work
- I took a ' Right-First-Time ' approach to my work
- I kept all relevant data, calendars, schedules handy
- I ensured data and equipment were updated regularly
- I took any important messages in writing
- I had any messages and numbers repeated and any unusual names spelled out and I wrote them down and had them repeated back
- I followed all procedures and standards

1. You worked on a till or did the petty cash. You were Miss Penny Perfect and often won the monthly shop award Best in Till management.
2. You worked with figures and NEVER had any work returned to you for correction.
3. You carefully measured or weighed or calculated things. You measured and fitted carpets. You measured wallpaper. You hate waste.
4. You carefully cut lengths of valuable materials, such as tiles, regal velvet curtains, carpets without mistakes or waste.
5. You monitored instruments, dials, meters or gauges.
6. You checked, inspected and did quality control.
7. You recorded details perfectly. You entered data onto a spreadsheet or database.
8. You copied and scanned important legal documents or similar financial ones.
9. You arranged items, such as a collection of books/CDs in strict alphabetical order.
10. You catalogued and filed papers/books meticulously to British Library standards.
11. You did stock ordering or stock control in a shop or warehouse.
12. You followed very strict guidelines, rules or procedures to the letter before repaying large amounts of money or refunds to customers.
13. You took the minutes of your team meetings. You then checked the accuracy. You then emailed them to all who attended for review and further

thoughts to be signed off as a true record. When done, you forwarded them to all relevant absentees and partners

14   You processed information / data in order to balance the equation/book.

15   You made a meticulous record of things.

16   You arranged catering, flight bookings, weddings or funerals and never made a mistake.

Example 17 : You worked in a call-centre taking emergency calls from people reporting gas leaks. You had to enter names, totally accurate addresses including postcodes and totally accurate phone numbers. You then had to give out accurate instructions to the caller. You then had to despatch the emergency gas workers. You had the caller repeat the address and phone numbers back to you and spell any unusual names. You were commended each year for your accuracy.

Example 18 : You worked in a Customer Services Department in an office and you noticed that many of the problems revolved around the staff recording the customers' emails slightly incorrectly : the letter O was often transcribed as the figure zero and the letter I was being written as the figure one. You suggested that everyone use the same phonetic alphabet. It was agreed and adopted. The number of errors fell by 40% in one year.

Example 19 : You had computer programming as a hobby. If you typed even one comma or full stop incorrectly, the program wouldn't run.

Example 20 : If you are school leaver and did the sciences, you can write how for example, your chemistry project was compromised if you had not assured the quality of the correct concentration of the ingredients . If you had not measured the powders / liquids exactly, you would have derived an erroneous result – or blown yourself up ! If you are a school leaver and did Sociology or Geography or Psychology, you can write how you had to ensure your statistics were solid or else your conclusions would have been invalid

Example 21 : When you cared for your granny, you carefully measured the dosage of her medicine. Never making a mistake.

Example 22. : When you worked in an office, one of your trusted colleagues was sending out invoices for seemingly random amounts, which baffled everyone. For example, a bill for fifty pounds was sent out as 350.00 and a bill for two hundred pounds was sent out as 3200.00 At first, a computer virus was suspected and then fraud. You noticed that in every case, the wrong figure always began with the figure '3'. You tested your colleague's keyboard and found that the' Shift' key was failing intermittently and needed replacing. Instead of typing the £ sign, it had sometimes failed and had typed the number 3 instead.

7.3 The Communication Competencies

The interviewer wants to be sure that you understood : that communication is a two-way process ; the need for rapport; the importance of active listening; the need to check mutual understanding; the need to speak in a structured manner; the need to adapt your communication style to suit the listener.

- I actively listened, giving my undivided attention - not interrupting, pre-judging, stereotyping, assuming or preparing my reply
- I established rapport and personalised the encounter, using their name, not account number
- I asked open and probing questions to gain info and understand needs and issues
- I explained why information was required
- I explained complex processes in a simple manner
- I used clear, concise, unambiguous language, avoiding jargon, slang or abbreviations
- I presented information in a structured, logical format and in context
- I pitched my language, content and style at the appropriate level for the listener
- I was positive and polite at all times
- I paused to allow him to contribute
- I checked my understanding
- I checked and confirmed *his* understanding via questioning
- I summarised my points to ensure clarity
- I kept focused on the issue in question
- I gave praise, thanks and constructive feedback
- I conveyed disappointing news with tact and sensitivity
- I shared ideas, information and feedback
- I relayed relevant info only to those needing to know it
- I provided knowledgeable and credible responses to queries

7.3.1   WRITTEN COMMUNICATION : all the above PLUS :

- I used a variety of illustrations (charts, graphs) to explain my points, if appropriate
- I used correct grammar, punctuation and spelling
- I organised my ideas clearly in a well-structed manner
- I wrote in a brief, clear and manner using appropriate style
- I provided examples and comparisons , if appropriate
- I checked emails / letters / reports had been received and understood
- I chose the right method of communication (email / letter / text / etc to address the recipient

7.3.2   PHONE COMPETENCIES : All the above plus :

- I was prepared with pen, paper & PC switched on, programmes open
- I had my calendar & necessary information at hand
- I was not eating, drinking or chewing
- I answered the phone promptly, within three rings
- I answered with a smile, enthusiasm and warmth
- I gave a greeting and identified myself
- I did not speak too quickly
- I considered time differences of the caller
- I considered possible disabilities of the caller
- I actively listened
- I individualised the call, using the caller's name
- I empathised, if appropriate
- I apologised, if appropriate
- I used appropriate questions - open, closed or probing
- I had the caller spell out any unusual names
- I checked the message I had taken
- If transferring, I first ensured the contact was available
- If transferring, I explained the reason to the caller and gave the contact's name
- If putting on hold, I asked caller's permission first
- I checked my understanding by short paraphrasing
- I followed up on any actions I had earlier promised to the caller

7.3.3. FACE-TO-FACE COMPETENCIES : all the above PLUS

- I watched for non-verbal clues such as body language and responded appropriately
- I responded with non-verbal actions (nods and smiles) to show my understanding
- I used a variety of media and graphic aids to reinforce my points and maintain interest
- I was conscious of cultural differences, such as personal space, touching and different body language messages

7.3.ex   26 Communication Examples :

1   You explained something to an elderly person or a young child – e.g how to use a PC, camera or phone.

2   You explained something complicated to a new work colleague, customer or neighbour. A rota. Timetable. Application-form. Test. Notice. Letter.

3   You gave a message to the public, perhaps over the tannoy.

4   You wrote a procedure guide for new members of staff.

5   You listened to a customer who had a complaint.

6   You took a message carefully and relayed it.

7   You wrote an important email or letter.

8   You gave a talk or presentation to a group.

9   You answered the phone.

10   You explained procedures to a new work colleague.

11   You met and greeted someone.

12   You took messages on a reception desk

13   You designed an advert / poster / flyer

14   You gave a speech - perhaps a best man speech.

15   You sold stuff at car-boot sale /shop /market stall / fete

16   You interviewed people

17   You befriended the elderly or the needy in a food bank

18   You helped kids to read

19   You took phone-calls from vulnerable students

20   You took part in the debating society

21   You acted in the drama group

22   You presented a show in the hospital or student radio

23   You spoke up at your local residents' association or Homewatch group

24   You participated in a Parent - Teacher forum

Example " Give me an example of when you have communicated something clearly to someone."

Example 25 :

At the Careers Office, I had to give a talk to neighbouring college about our services. I prepared by investigating my target audience by phoning the college tutor to find the make-up of the class : their age-group, background, course and aspirations and what they sought from this talk.

I then considered my style of communication (simple but not condescending) , my content and my presentation (whether to use PowerPoint, video, flipcharts, etc.). Finding the class to be 20 students, I suggested a short video followed by a 10-15 minute talk by me, aided by using flipcharts, followed by a Q&A session. She agreed.

I explained to the class what we would do. While speaking, I used vocabulary which was appropriate to that age and client group. I avoided using jargon, abbreviations or slang. To maintain interest, I used various techniques : I used humour; I paced my speech with pauses, knowing that people have different attention spans; and I alternated my speech with the images on the flowcharts. To help them remember what I said, I used repetition, linking, reinforcement and summarization. After handing out leaflets, I held a Question and Answer session.

The result of the talk was that the Q & A session was very lively and spontaneous, with the students wanting to know much more about our services. The other result was that the college tutor was so impressed that she arranged for the careers visits to become a regular feature at the college.

Notice how some of the indicators of the competency were included in the answer..... investigated the target audience and its needs.... considered my style, content and presentation .....explained in advance what would happen .... avoided jargon, abbreviations and slang... paced my speech with pauses ...alternated my speech with images.......to aid memory, I used repetition, linking, reinforcement and summarization....... checked understanding.

7.4 The Customer Service Competencies

The interviewer is looking to see that you displayed the range of interpersonal skills needed to service customers with excellence, including establishing rapport; active listening; transparency; checking mutual understanding; balancing of needs; managing expectations; over-delivering; taking responsibility for the whole enquiry / complaint/ transaction. " Going the extra mile" (doing more than the bare minimum).

- I established rapport and personalised the encounter, using his name, not account number
- I cleverly established the customer's hierarchy of needs with suitable questioning
- I actively listened - not interrupting, pre-judging, assuming or mentally preparing my response
- I checked my understanding of the customer's situation and needs by paraphrasing or summarizing and then checked he had understood me
- I empathized with the customer's situation
- I communicated clearly, avoiding jargon, slang and abbreviations, so as not to confuse him.
- I pitched my language/content/style at the appropriate level
- I considered any special needs such as age, disability, health, cultural background, literacy or language
- I presented him with a range of appropriate options and alternatives
- I tactfully balanced his needs with the business needs
- I was honest and transparent as to our policies
- I managed his unrealistic expectations
- I protected the customer's security, confidentiality and privacy
- I remained patient, helpful, professional and polite at all times
- I was positive at all times and conveyed bad news with sensitivity
- I sought assistance if I was unable to resolve the problem
- I explained my processes and time-scales to avoid call-backs
- I continually updated myself with the latest policies, products
- I delivered excellent customer service by being an expert at my job
- I ensured the customer was happy with the resolution
- I took responsibility for the customer's problem/complaint or wishes
- I solicited the customer's level of satisfaction at the end
- I followed up on actions that I had promised or on his enquiries
- I considered how feedback and complaints could improve my service
- I under-promised , then over-delivered
- I went the extra mile: that is, I did more than the minimum
- I gave a customised service, not lip-service
- I aimed for a 'Right-First-Time' approach when dealing with customers
- I proactively sensed when a customer needed help and didn't wait to be asked to give it.

7.4   ex   18 Customer Service Examples :

1. You worked in a shop or a market stall or on a delivery round
2. You worked in a call centre
3. You worked on a helpdesk
4. You worked in the library for two weeks as work experience
5. You worked as an unpaid volunteer in a charity shop
6. You worked weekends or during the summer holidays in your uncle's shop
7. You helped out at your local school or church fete
8. You held your own jumble sales, garage sales or yard sales
9. You manned the phones at charity begathons
10. You handled complaints. You dealt with demanding, irate customers
11. You gave someone a lift. You went the extra mile in some way.

Give an example of when you have given excellent Customer Service" **Ex 12**

When I worked in a shop, I was deputising for the manager one Saturday. The security guard came over with an old woman who said she had put her bag down and someone stolen it. She was crying, very distressed and frightened .

I took her into the office, established rapport with her by asking her name and giving mine, sat her down and asked her if she would like a cup of tea. I got the security guard to rustle one up for up for her. I got all the relevant info from her by getting her to tell me exactly what had happened. I actively listened, by not interrupting , judging or assuming anything. I empathized with her , saying the shock must have been awful and I checked my understanding as to what had happened.

I took into consideration her special needs : she was hard of hearing and elderly and so I spoke clearly, slowly and loudly. I explained our processes and asked her if she wanted to involve the Police, which she did. I called the Police and before they took her home, I asked if there was anything else we could do for her. We had no CCTV at that time. Thankfully, her keys were not in her bag and I asked her if I could call on her after work to check that she was okay. That afternoon, I organised a collection for her from the neighbouring shops in our mall and raised twice as much as the money that she had in her bag. I called on her later that day with a colleague and she was overjoyed.

The result was that she became a regular customer and told all her friends about what we had done for her. The story actually made the local paper. We gained about 5% new customers after that good publicity. I recommended to my manager that we get CCTV and she arranged it .

Note she included **some** competency **indicators of Customer Service**
...established rapport... gathered all the relevant info... actively listened
.empathized.... checked understanding......took into consideration special
needs ...explained processes...asked if there was anything else we could do for
her. She went the extra mile by organizing a collection and calling in on her.
Notice too that she quantified the success by giving a percentage. **" Give me**
an example of when you have resolved a customer's complaint or handled
an irate customer. " Example 13 :

When I was working in an electricals shop, a woman came in who was very
angry complaining that a washing-machine she had bought from us had
broken down again after only two weeks.

I let her vent, not taking things personally and then empathised, saying it must
have been very frustrating for her. I apologised for what had happened and
then I established all the facts by effectively questioning her. I actively listened,
by not interrupting or judging or assuming. She said it had broken down twice
already. I checked my understanding by paraphrasing.

I reminded myself not to argue or be defensive. I remembered that we had
already had several complaints over that model . I asked her what she wanted
the outcome to be and I tactfully balanced her needs with the business needs
by explaining to her what we could and couldn't do : we could replace it with a
new one, refund her money or have it mended with a reduction on her
payments. She wanted to buy a slightly more expensive model made by a
different manufacturer. I explained the situation to my Team Leader and
suggested that considering the circumstances, as a goodwill gesture, we allow
her to exchange her machine.

He agreed. I checked that the customer understood and was happy with the
proposal and for installation the next day. I put it in writing , we all signed up
and I arranged the delivery and installation. We had a letter a month later
from her saying she was thrilled with her new washing-machine and was
recommending us to her neighbours, which brought us 5% more sales in the
next quarter.

I am being told often by email that the 3 most common questions asked on
Customer Service in 2018 are : 1 - Give me an example of how you have
handled a difficult customer. 2 - Give me an example of how you have handled
a complaint. 3 - Give me an example of how you have gone the extra mile for a
customer.

There are many subtle skills involved in handling a very angry customer, when he is in front of you. The general principles include :

1   Take him away from his audience.
2   Get him to sit down.
3   Apologise to him.
4   Promise him your honesty.
5   Identify with him and show empathy.
6   Get him to vent his anger slowly - by having him repeat the problem, by your active listening and by your paraphrasing of it.
7   Ask him what he wants the outcome to be.
8   Give him the options.

Take him away from his audience because often, angry people play up to their friends, partners or family in a show of bravado. They use their friends as support. Their friends might even encourage them or stir them up to further anger. The customer will not like to lose face in front of them. Take him away from them to another part of the office or at least to a desk from which they cannot approach.

The reason for getting someone to sit down is twofold : angry people calm down much quicker when they are seated and also it is more difficult for them to headbutt you or attack you in other ways.

Apologise in a non-commital but sincere way. Don't admit that your organisation has done something. Instead, say " I'm sorry, something has obviously gone wrong" and then you immediately promise to do all in your power to resolve the matter and give your name in full and even offer your direct line number. You will be amazed how much a simple apology both calms many people and also elicits their co-operation. Being defensive or whitewashing a problem only aggravates matters.

If possible, identify with his situation. Show empathy by saying " I had something very similar happen to me last year and it was horrible". Don't say " I know what it's like", since all situations are different and it could come over as patronising and inflame the matter.

He will probably have shouted out half the story to you already but you need to establish the full facts and you will need to do it carefully and skillfully. The way to proceed is to say " Okay Mr Smith, can I check that I've got this right ? You bought this from us / you were told to ...... blah blah" .....and then get him to retell his story again from the beginning. This will both help him to calm down, since he is expelling more air but it will also help you get the story right. You need to be careful when deciding to ask him to repeat his narrative because this can further enrage some potentially violent people.

You must watch his body language –forming a fist or gritting his teeth - and listen to his breathing. Watch for micro-movements of his mouth and eyes.

If a customer is still swearing or threatening you, you must lay down limits by saying " Mr Smith, I really do want to sort this out for you but I can't work, when I'm being sworn at or threatened". If he continues, get up and walk away but do so safely.

Go through the incident with him, checking your understanding to determine what really happened. Paraphrase it (that is, repeat it back to him briefly and ensure he agrees your understanding is correct). Ask him what he wants the outcome to be. Empower him by giving options, if appropriate.

Example 14 :

When I worked in the Jobcentre, a customer came in effin and blinding about the non-arrival of his giro and yelling that his kids were starving because of the heartless, brutal fascists in the Jobcentre.

The first thing I did was to let him vent for a while, as this helps angry people get their anger out of their system. I then asked him to come to my desk to remove him from his friends, as I could sense that a lot of his venom was bravado to impress his friends. It also made it harder for him if he wanted to attack me.

I apologised, saying that something had obviously gone wrong and I promised to do everything in my power to sort out the problem, freely giving my full name and direct line number. Having someone apologise pleasantly surprised and even shocked him and he calmed down a bit. When I told him that the same thing had happened to me a couple of times when I used to sign on at the Jobcentre and it was horrible, he calmed down a bit more.

Seeing that he was starting to be reasonable, I told him that I wanted to make sure that I had understood everything correctly. I asked him to repeat what had happened. I listened very carefully, not assuming or prejudging and I then asked a couple of questions to ascertain the full facts. I asked him if I had got things right.

It turned out that he had forgotten that he had not signed on two days previously as he ought to have and that had caused this delay. I assured him the giro had been sent out and if he did not receive it today, I would make a counter payment for him. He grudgingly apologised to me for calling me a **** and left. As he did, a customer came in effin and blinding about ....

Example 15 : An irate customer phoned complaining his order had still not arrived. I investigated and found that his address had been incorrectly recorded and so the order had been returned. I took his correct details and got permission from my Team Leader to arrange a 25% discount as an apology and goodwill gesture

Example 16 : When a customer came into the shop and his size of shoe was not available, I phoned a neighbouring branch, which had his size in. Since the customer was a tourist who was soon to catch a plane later that day and didn't know our town, I volunteered to walk there to get it for him. I went the extra mile. Well, quarter-mile !

Example 17 : I worked in an optician's. I went out of my way to drop off a pair of glasses at a customer's house on my way home from work, so that her young daughter could have her glasses for her school exam the next morning.

Example 18 : I was a taxi-driver. I took a family to an airport. I made a 10 mile return journey, at no extra charge, to collect a child's teddy bear she had left at the hotel. I didn't go the extra mile, I went the extra 10 miles.

When answering Customer Care questions, always include the fact that you **ensured mutual understanding**. If you don't, you will probably fail. We always assume that we have perfectly understood what the customer has told us and then we assume that the customer has perfectly understood what we told them. Very often, we have misunderstood and so have they.

If possible and if appropriate, always try to include the fact that you **involved the customer in the resolution** of any dispute - you asked you gave them options.

7.5   The Deadlines and Targets Competencies

The interviewer needs to know you understood the importance of prioritizing, planning and building in contingency time. He wants to know the lengths you went to to achieve your targets and meet your deadlines.

This competency is all about finishing all of your work, on time and to the expected standards. For this competency, you need to show that you understand the importance of taking responsibility for getting all your work done within the agreed timescales. How do you ensure that ? You use the

APPLE system for meeting deadlines and targets. **A=Assess P=Prioritize P=Plan L=Launch E=Evaluate**

In your example, you must show the lengths you went to, in order to achieve your targets and meet your deadlines. You must show how you overcame setbacks and delays to your plans to fulfil your contracts with no loss of quality in your work.

- I queried the deadline
- I renegotiated and extended / re-scheduled the deadline
- I assessed my workload / project
- I prioritized the tasks into Urgent, Important and Non-Urgent
- I planned my objectives using the SMARTER model (Objectives must be Specific, Measurable, Realistic, Timebound, Evaluated, Re-Evaluated)
- I built in some contingency time to allow for delays and emergencies
- I set my deadline earlier than the real one, building in overrun and checking time
- I enlisted help from colleagues and friends in exchange for future return favours
- I carefully and appropriately delegated some work to others, if necessary
- I monitored and evaluated my progress and objectives regularly
- I used To-Do lists, diaries, calendars and alarms
- I used a Brought/ Forward system, if necessary, to ensure nothing was missed
- I usefully employed downtime such as waiting time, travelling times etc.
- I worked overtime / came in early/ stayed late / worked weekends.
- I worked at home, if that was needed, to meet my targets or deadlines
- I focused on the desired outcomes
- I used the most suitable methods to get the job done

Two cars have collided head on and a doctor, who happens to be driving by, stops to attend to the wounded. Should he dash in and treat the first victim he sees ? Should he treat the man he saw first , who is hobbling and who might have a broken ankle or should he treat the woman who can't breathe ? You know the answer.

The first thing you must do in any of your work is to stop for a moment and **TAKE STOCK** of the situation and not just charge headlong into it. In other words, you must **ASSESS YOUR WORKLOAD** for the day and its deadlines.

Then you must **PRIORITIZE** it into work which is Urgent, then work which is Important and then work which is just Routine. It's that simple. Obviously, you start doing the Urgent work first ! Prioritizing your work is such a vital component to efficiency and you MUST include it , both in the example you give and at your interview or you will fail. It is impossible to "Deliver at Pace" without it.

Then you must the **PLAN YOUR DAY** by assigning a certain amount of work per hour (eg you will process 5 applications per hour until 12 noon or manufacture 100 pots per hour or phone 6 customers per hour, etc.). You will then allow for unforeseen things such as interruptions or emergencies with some **CONTINGENCY TIME** (perhaps 15 mins per day). You can use the 'SMARTER model to plan your objectives : ensure they are Specific, Measurable, Achievable, Realistic, Timebound, Evaluated and Re-Evaluated.

You **LAUNCH** into it, meaning that you avoid procrastination and faffing around.

At regular intervals, perhaps when the clock strikes hourly, you **EVALUATE** your progress against your plan and make approriate adjustments, if you are falling behind schedule. Monitoring your progress regularly is vital.

It's as easy as an **APPLE.**

7.5   ex   14 Deadlines and Targets Examples

1. You completed work by a certain time.
2. You submitted an essay or coursework for college by a certain date.
3. You completed work for a customer by a set time.
4. You repaired/ serviced a car or machine for a customer for a set date.
5. You prepared a report for a meeting.
6. You met your sales targets in order to receive your commission or pay.
7. You paid your bills on time.
8. You learned your lines for a play or learned a piece of music for a recital.
9. You organised a function, kids' party, a wedding, fete or a funeral

"Give me an example of when you have had to work to a deadline"

Example 10:

A sudden job offer meant moving from my flat within 7 days or lose the job. It was full of my treasured belongings - books, CDs and furniture, which I had to pack or sell off. It meant hard decisions and a lot of work within a tight deadline.

Firstly, I queried the deadline, renegotiated it and had it extended by 2 days. I then analysed all my jobs and the time and the resources I had available. I would have to contact all the utility companies, the council, the doctor, my landlord, the Royal Mail, the removal company and host of other parties too.

After careful thinking, I prioritized all the jobs into Urgent, Important and Routine.

I then planned my objectives using the SMARTER model (i.e. ensuring my objectives were Specific, Measurable, Achievable, Realistic, Timebound, Evaluated and Re-evaluated). I estimated a certain amount of time per task but I also built in contingency time to allow for delays and unknowns.

I enlisted help from friends , who helped after work and all day on moving day and I carefully delegated appropriate tasks to them. I kept monitoring the work's progress and objectives on a daily basis using a B/F system in my diary and on an hourly basis. I donated half my stuff to charity and packed half.

The result was that I managed to move in time with only one or two small breakages. The whole experience reinforced for me the necessity of good planning.

Example 11 : You worked late or through your lunch or at weekends in order to meet your deadlines.

Note how he included some of the all-important competency indicators of Delivering at Pace : ...prioritized into Urgent, Important and Routine ......planned my objectives using the SMARTER model...........built contingency time .....reviewed and evaluated work regularly.....used a B/F (brought-forward) system.........employed downtime

Example 12 : Frank had a small company of computer programmers. They were planning to launch a new game when they read that a competitor was about to bring out a similar one just before their own. Therefore, Frank decided to ask his team if they would postpone their holidays and all work longer to get the project completed ahead of schedule. They did, the launch was a great success, they took the market share that their competitor might have taken and they became a better team because of it.

Example 13 :

When studying for my NVQ3in Computing, I had no PC. I had to complete all the modules, gather the evidence and have it assessed within a tight 13-week timescale, all while sharing computers. I knew this would require good planning and self-discipline.

I prioritized the modules then planned my objectives using the SMARTER model.   I allocated so many modules per week, using weekly and daily To-Do lists. I factored in an extra 10% contingency time, in case of sickness or delays. I booked a PC for the times I needed one for the first month and set reminders for the rest.

I used a B/F system in my pocket diary to ensure no uncompleted assignment was missed and I evaluated my progress each day and altered my plans, if needed. I worked steadily and consistently and kept my objective and deadline in mind at all times. I pre-empted distractions and interruptions by telling friends not to call me or visit at certain times; by keeping conversations brief; by turning off my phone and by not answering my door, if needed.

I prevented procrastination by breaking difficult modules down into smaller, more manageable chunks and by reminding myself of the potential reward and consequences of failure.

The outcome was that, due to good planning, frequent monitoring, awareness of deadlines and self-discipline, I comfortably completed all the modules , had them assessed on time and I gained my desired qualification.

Refer also to the Managing Yourself competency, 8.4, since that too can involve meeting deadlines.
In an interview, be sure to say that you assessed your work in hand, prioritized it, planned it and monitored it regularly. If you don't, you will certainly fail.

"Tell me of a time when you have worked to deadlines"
Example 14 :

When I worked in the mailroom of a finance company, I worked alone and I had to be on top of the inflow and despatch at all times. I was told it had not gone well in the past.

For the first incoming delivery, I had to open, count, weigh, sort and record all incoming mail. I had to record all the Recorded and Special Delivery items and cheques, Postal Orders and all certificates. I had date-stamp everything and scan the certificates to the email boxes of their caseworkers. All mail had to be sorted, assigned and delivered to the caseworker or department by 10 am. Returning at 10-45 with outgoing mail I had picked up from the designated points I insisted on, I repeated the process for the second delivery, again collecting all outgoing mail as I was delivering the incoming mail.

After a short lunch, I began to complete the Royal Mail online and Parcelforce bags along with the private courier bags, books and online work for the private couriers such as TNT and DHL. I franked all the letters and completed the recorded and special delivery books. I had set my alarm to sound at each hour and half-hour mark and at those times, I did a quick run round collecting all outgoing mail and parcels. I imposed a deadline on staff for "In the Out Baskets by 4pm", giving me 30 mins to finally complete the online documents, seal the courier bags and do all final counts and recordings.

Because (a) I was very well organised with my routine and always well stocked with stationery (b) I made regular collection runs (thanks to my alarm clock alerts and (c) I had the staff understand their responsibilities, I always met my deadlines of getting the caseworkers' post to them on time and getting all post out to the customers on time.

This competency question is increasingly becoming more important as employers are assessing whether a robot would be more capable and reliable in meeting deadlines and delivering on targets. If asked if you have ever missed your deadlines, always say 'No'. You can say that you came close once, when there was an unexpected surge but you told your boss immediately, who dropped what he was doing to give you a hand and so you met your deadline. I was once told by someone, who had an interview with a funeral insurance company, that even they had deadlines to meet. ☺

7.6   The Decision Making Competencies

This competency involves showing the employer that you followed an excellent decision-making model to go forward, rather than making your mind up impulsively, randomly or lazily. You need to show that your decisions are based on EVIDENCE and logical method rather than guesswork or intuition and they are based on DATA rather than assumptions. Stating that your decision-making model involves tossing a coin won't do !

You need to show that you identified your objective, gathered relevant information, evaluated it, generated viable options, critically evaluated the pros, cons and risks and only then made a good decision, which you were ready to modify. I repeat : you must show that you based your decision on data / evidence, not emotion, prejudice or assumption.

We always make better decision in lfe when we are better informed. In your example, you must show that you were well-informed — you gathered lots of info and ensured it was relevant, current, impartial , credible and complete. It must be from reputable, verifiable sources.

You must show that you critically appraised and analysed it by comparing like for like. (i) You can't compare apples with pears (ii) you must be aware of your own conscious and unconscious biases (iii) you must be aware of how stats can be distorted to deceive.

You must filter to get a shortlist of options and consider the potential consequences of each before reaching your final decision. Your example must show your decision was objective and arrived at through reason, not emotion or bias.

In terms of competencies, the interviewer is ensuring you can make well-informed and timely decisions, and that you perceive the impact, implications and potential consequences of decisions you may make.

- I identified my specific objective =what decision had to be made and why
- I collected as much info as possible, from a wide variety of sources
- I ensured the data was current and sources were reputable
- I sorted the relevant from the irrelevant, important from non-important
- I organised the material in a way that aided analysis , like for like, and extracted it appropriately

- I identified and investigated gaps, inconsistencies and ambiguities
- I critically appraised the evidence
- I generated realistic options and discarded unrealistic ones
- I filtered the options into a shortlist
- I assessed the pros, cons, risks and potential consequences of each remaining option
- I confirmed my understanding
- I knew my limitations and involved others with relevant expertise, if necessary
- I made my objective and impartial decision based on the evidence, not emotion, assumption, gossip, hearsay, rumour, guesswork, bias, advertising or incomplete data
- After implementation, I evaluated my decision and confirmed/revised it, taking corrective action based on feedback
- I introduced quality assurance checks, where appropriate.

7.6   ex 20 Decision Making Examples

1. You decided to buy any expensive item, such as a house or car or TV.
2. You had to decide whether to buy or rent a home.
3. You decided which school to send your children to.
4. You had to decide which hospital to go to.
5. You had to decide which insurance plan / policy to take out or renew.
6. You had to decide between several job offers.
7. You had to decided between several financial investments / savings.
8. You decided which contractor to hire for a job in your home.
9. You had to make a decision over which university/course to attend.
10. You had to decide whether to emigrate or not.
11. You had to decide to relocate or not.
12. You had to decide between various offers, such as bank loans.
13. You had to decide between a number of job offers
14. You decided to switch bank accounts.
15. You decided to buy-to-let
16. You decided to opt for part-rent, part-mortgage.
17. You decided to change broadband, mobile phone or utility supplier.
18. You decided on a pension scheme

"Give me an example of when you have had to make a major decision."

Example 19 :

A while back, although I had access to a computer at work, I realised that I needed a computer at home . I wasn't sure whether to buy a PC or a laptop. It was a major expenditure and since I couldn't afford to make a mistake, I so had to ensure that I made the right decision.

The first thing I did was I identified my specific objective (buy a computer) and my specific needs - immediate, medium and long term. I asked myself how I would use it mostly. - writing ? music ? family webchats ? How much speed and storage would I need and how soon would it be obsolete. I then collected as much relevant information as I needed from a wide variety of sources, ensuring the info was up-to-date (brochures in shops, websites, chatrooms, consumer groups, independent reviews). I then consulted with computer-shop assistants, friends and work colleagues for advice.

After organising the material in a way that would help analysis and extracting the relevant info appropriately, I generated realistic options for my budget, which led me to decide on a laptop. I filtered the options to a shortlist of three (based on spec, length of guarantee, IT support and price). After assessing the pros and cons and risks of each and confirming my understanding (by emailing the companies), I then made my well-informed and objective decision.

The outcome was that I bought a laptop which served my needs perfectly. I never regretted my decision once and later saw that model go on to win many awards.

Notice he included the competency indicators of Decision Making and these must always be stated in the correct order ....*I .identified my specific objective and needs... I collected as much relevant information as needed ...from a wide variety of sources..... ensuring it was up-to-date....I consulted for advice ..... I organised the material in a way that would help analysis and extracted it appropriately....I generated realistic options... I filtered the options to a shortlist...I assessed the pros and cons and risks of each option I confirmed my understanding. I made my decision.*   (This decision-making model should be used for any decision you have made. In your example, you may need to add that you evaluated and then later re-evaluated your decision as you worked, but it wasn't appropriate here.)

- **Example 20**.......You received some money in a will and wanted to invest it. You researched all the bank & building society accounts, online and off and other options such as Premium Bonds, Fixed Rate Bonds, etc. You evaluated the pros, cons and risks of all of them.

After writing your answer, re-read the first three paragraphs of 7.6 and also re-read the Decision Making Competencies and check that your answer includes the advice given in them.

Above all, be sure to say your decision was based on EVIDENCE , whose data was reliable, broad and current and that you carefully evaluated the PROS, CONS, RISKS and POTENTIAL CONSEQUENCES of your decision.

Decision making is often similar to problem solving, so please now read the Problem Solving Competencies, 8.7

7.7 The Drive, Determination or Resilience Competencies

The interviewer wants to hear how you kept going despite resistance or obstacles. How you persevered. How you recovered from a serious setback.

- I adopted a positive and thankful approach

- I used the " SMARTER " technique – (Specific, Measurable, Achievable, Realistic, Timebound, Evaluated, Re-Evaluated) to set my goals

- I broke the task down into small, bite-size chunks

- I rewarded myself after completing each small unit

- I surrounded myself with motivational quotes and family photos

- I prevented interruptions – I told friends when not to call, tactfully curtailed conversations and switched off my phone.

- I prevented procrastination – by breaking tasks down into smaller chunks

7.7 ex   14 Drive, Determination or Resilience Examples :

1. You recovered from a bad accident - maybe you learned to walk again.
2. You recovered from a messy, long divorce
3. You recovered from a protracted legal matter
4. You recovered from a redundancy
5. You recovered from bankruptcy
6. You recovered from a devastating bereavement
7. You finally had a baby after a very long course of IVF treatment
8. You traced your family tree after much effort
9. You tracked down someone , perhaps your real parent, after much work
10. You passed your exams, despite missing some time due to illness
11. You fought a long, exhausting campaign and won
12. You did not give up on a resolution - you gave up smoking or lost weight.
13. You had been out of work for a long time and were looking for shop work. There was not much of it about but you persevered by dropping your CV personally in every shop in a 4 mile radius , every 4 weeks until you were successful.
14. You were so driven that you relocated to find work.

7.8   The Equality and Diversity Competencies

The interviewer wants to be sure you were comfortable working with people from a range of diverse ages, sexualities, backgrounds and abilities.

Equality and Diversity isn't only about racial equality. It isn't solely about skin tone or nationality. It includes how we treat those with a disability, those younger or older than ourselves, those with a different religion or sexual preference to ours and anyone who we feel is different to us.

We can consciously and overtly discriminate against people we don't like. We can choose to treat someone unfavourably if we don't like redheads, for example. We stereotype new people and categorise them almost instantly on first impressions of them to see if they are "like us or not". We can dislike someone for the clothes they wear, their accent, their weight and so on. It's grossly unfair and simply stupid of us. You don't necessarily have to agree with another person's lifestyle : you just have to know about it and be comfortable working with people who are different than you. If you can't, there is no place for you in the workplace.

However, we discriminate against others every day in unconscious ways too. This is known as **UNCONSCIOUS BIAS** and the usual types of this are :

AFFINITY BIAS – we favour others we feel we have a bond with (maybe they share an interest of ours)

CONFIRMATORY BIAS – we favour them because they say things which confirm or reaffirm our beliefs or we disfavour them because they just happen to confirm a bias of ours (example – you are holding interviews and an overweight candidate arrives 2 minutes late : it "confirms" your belief that "All fat people are lazy" and you don't give them a fair interview.

CONFORMITY BIAS - This is the 'bandwagon' bias, in that your view is wrongly swayed by others around you. You are afraid to be seen as different, so you go along with everyone else.

HALO BIAS – we favour someone based on a particular characteristic or trait that we admire.

Two lesser, more subtle biases are :

ATTRIBUTION BIAS - We make assumptions about people and then we attribute reasons and intentions to their behaviour, awarding positive attributes to those we feel are "like us" and negative attributions to those who feel are not. We don't know much about someone or a certain situation, so we guess or make assumptions and jump to conclusions.

AVAILABILITY BIAS – We quickly decide upon the easiest, most likely explanation for something, right or wrong.

These biases lead to cliques, exclusion and segregation, even if not intended.

- I treated everyone with respect and dignity. D.I.V.E.R.S.I.T.Y means **D**iferent **I**ndividuals **V**aluing **E**ach other, **R**egardless of Race, Religion, **S**kin, **S**exuality,, **I**ntellect , **T**alents or **Y**ears.

- I respected all differences in race, gender, age, ethnic background, sexual orientation, disabilities, carer levels and opinions

- I watched my stereotypical responses and prejudices

- I tried at al times to aware of my unconscious bias

- I tried to work with as wide a range of people as possible

- I learned about the customs and norms of others

- I remembered that different cultures have different norms about personal space

- I was aware that humour and the appropriateness of humour differs in different cultures

- I learned that body language messages differ in different cultures – such as nodding, waving one's head, using a thumb's up sign, winking

- I learned that different cultures have different norms around eye contact

- I took an interest in the background of others

- I was open and willing to listen to other viewpoints

- I promoted inclusion by supporting initiatives and programs to increase my understanding of diversity

- I enrolled on equality and diversity courses, such as the Disability Discrimination Acts and Equality in the Workplace.

- I avoided making assumptions based on his accent or appearance

- I acted when seeing or hearing someone being discriminated against

- When I stood in for my Team Leader for a month, I realised the difficulties that colleagues with children had over the timetable schedules. I recommended a flexi-time work system to my bosses and also a part-time work system, which was later adopted.

7.8ex   17 Equality and Diversity examples

Example 1 :

When working in Personnel, I was asked to lead a team of four to recruit 30 staff for a new project. I chose my team to be as diverse and inclusive in terms of age, race and ability as possible.

I ensured that the posts were advertised widely and openly and that they stated they were available to anyone with the minimum qualifications we needed (five good GCSEs).

The department policy was that competency questions would be used . I gave a great deal of thought as to how I could ensure that each application was treated on merit and so I suggested that in order to pre-empt unconscious bias, we use specific criteria to objectively compare candidate's abilities and to use a consistent rating system to score their application forms. I suggested that all names be hidden from the forms before they reached us and this was agreed.

After the 750 or so applications had been sifted down to around 250, I then suggested that we swap the forms amongst ourselves and repeat the sift, as a way of peer review. (A second opinion) . This was another way of removing any **unconscious bias** in our choices. The 250 were sifted down to around 80, who would be called to an interview.

I ordered it so that there would be three interviewers and that once again, specific criteria checklists and scoring lists were used to assess the candidates fairly.

The result was that , as much as possible, individual biases of the interviewers were precluded from the recruitment process. All new starters performed well in their contracts and I was commended by my manager both for the quality of staff recruited and also for rebalancing a glaring imbalance in diversity in the office. It was not an exercise in positive action but simply acting fairly by awarding jobs on merit, which ended up with the office more truly reflecting the local community, who employed it.

Example 2 : You volunteered to go on Equality/Diversity courses.

Example 3 : You mixed with diverse races at school or uni or at work or in the block or street where you live.

Example 4 :

When working as a volunteer community worker, I noticed the two sons of a recently arrived Iraqi refugee neighbour always watching our village under-11s team play football but never being invited to play or train with them. They always came in their shorts but wore only old, cheap trainers.

Thinking that they may have been ignored, I found out that they and their parents spoke no English and couldn't ask for a trial. I then spoke with a couple of the team coaches and asked if they could be allowed to join in with the boys at training. I explained that it only fair and better for all if we had a village that was inclusive and used the skills of everyone.

It turned out that they had simply had not realised that the refugee kids wanted to play. The two kids were invited to the next training session. I discreetly found that they had no boots and so the team coach asked some of the players to bring along their old ones.

The two kids turned out to be fantastic players, enriching the team and helping it to win its first trophy ever. The kids found out all about their past life in Iraq and their customs and adventures. The coaches did the same with the parents, everyone becoming lifelong friends and mutually benefitting. Their mother, an experienced weaver, shared her rare skills among her new friends.

I had shown leadership by stepping in to ensure inclusion.

Example 5 : You learned the culture of your ethnic neighbours

Example 6 : You stepped in to prevent homophobic bullying.

Example 7 : You covertly recorded a work colleague's anti-Scouser harassment of a Liverpudlian colleague and gave it as evidence in a tribunal, which got him dismissed.

Example 8 : You suggested an interpreter service at work

Example 9 : You looked after your disabled colleague, who was wheelchair bound, when the fire-alarms went off.

Example 10 : You had a sensitive, tactful regard for customers who were unable to read or write, helping to getting remedial help for them.

Example 11 : You volunteered as a Literacy Tutor

Example 12 : When you worked on your uncle's market stall, you took things from the back of the tables to the front so that disabled people in wheelchairs could more easily see and handle them. It resulted in an increase of sales of around 20% that year.

0-0-0-0-0-0

Under the Equality Act (which took over from the Disability Discrimination Act and the Race Relations Act), an employer is legally bound to make **"reasonable adjustments"** for disabled people to enable them to do their job or get a job. It also applies to any person or organisation serving a disabled customer.

Example 13 :

Although I had heard of Equality and Diversity, I wasn't aware that I had a legal duty concerning " reasonable adjustments ", so I went on a course about it.

I learned that : 1. I had a legal duty to remove barriers which prevented access to good service for a disabled person and I could be prosecuted if I did not. 2. The customer need not put his request for a reasonable adjustment in writing 3. The request had to be recorded. 4. The customer need not use the actual term 'reasonable adjustment'. 5. I could not ask for medical evidence of the disability , except in exceptional circumstances. 6. I have an anticipatory duty to make the adjustments so that they are ready and in good working order before the customer arrives. 7. I learned that some of the many simple adjustments included : providing a chair that can be altered in different ways; screen filters and risers to lift computer screens; filters for overhead lights; hearing loops/ amplified phones; having a sign language expert; having a translator; disabled toilets; external and internal ramps for wheelchairs; providing large font or Braille documents; Talktype keyboards.

The result was that the course gave me a much better understanding of the legislation and the difficulties that the disabled face.

Example 14 : After the council decided to integrate a special school with your school, there was an influx of disabled kids in your class. After seeing them struggling in different ways, you suggested that two of the desks be rearranged, so that a girl with a hearing impairment could see someone approaching her and not be taken by surprise; that the printer be put on a lower table, so that two wheelchair-users could more readily access it; the shelves on the wall be lowered so that the books be more easily reached for them; that a boy who had difficulty typing be given voice recognition software and be allowed to submit his essays by voice-to-type dictation .

These small reasonable adjustments cost very little but went someway to ensuring equality of opportunities for those kids.

Example 15 :

When Susan held a performance review with Chen, she told him that his work had fallen below the targets set. She was upset when he would not look at her and started smiling. She felt that he was being disrespectful.

When she mentioned this to her boss, Mei, who is Asian like Chen, she was informed that in his culture, it was very embarrassing to be told that your work was not up to standard and that not making eye contact was not a sign of disrespect but embarrassment and shame.

She also said that his smiling was the same. It was a way of relieving embarrassment and she said that some even made jokes when they were rebuked for poor work. She explained that it was a cultural thing , accepted and not seen as disrespectful at all but a way of coping with his humiliation.

Susan said she had no idea and decided to find out more about different cultural responses.

Example 16 : When you noticed your wheelchair-bound customers struggle (after they had crossed the road and approached your shop) , you asked the council to lower the kerb in front of your shop. They did and you gained around 15% more customers in the first six months alone.

Example 17 : When you worked for a well-known High Street budget fashion retail chain, it had just received national coverage for the shocking way its garment workers in Asia were being treated in their factories. When the management asked for volunteers to go there to run training workshops in anti-sexism, anti-homophobia, anti-racism and pro-disability etc you put yourself forward. It was a great opportunity to experience other cultures in their own lands and you really helped to improve the lives and working conditions, at least of those workers.

Chapter 8

8.1 The Initiative Competencies

The interviewer wants to see if you had to be told to act, when you saw a problem. He wants to know if you have ever had any ideas to improve methods . He wants to see if you just always sat around waiting to be told what to do.

- I sought additional challenges and responsibilities, doing more than the minimum

- I anticipated and predicted customer needs

- I pre-empted potential problems by anticipating them

- I took appropriate action before being forced by circumstances.

- I acted quickly in a crisis

- I generated new ideas, suggested new innovations before being asked

- I designed new ideas, systems, templates for improvement

- I recognized and took advantage of opportunities to improve our company's productivity

8.1   ex 16 Initiative Examples :

1. You recognized opportunities, seized them and used them to your advantage..
2. You saw a chance to save our company money/ increase sales or cut waste.
3. You volunteered for extra work, when the company was struggling.
4. You noticed a potential problem - a health and safety issue and took action to prevent an accident before it occurred . Wet floor ? Dangerous mat or lead ?
5. You foresaw potential difficulties and took pre-emptive action in time.
6. You noticed a recurring problem & acted before being asked to remedy it.

7. You acted quickly in a crisis, such as when someone was hurt in work. You were the one to call the doctor or administer First Aid or similar.
8. You took the initiative to improve your company's working practices, by submitting a suggestion / inventing something/ redesigning something.
9. You anticipated a customer's needs. A customer bought a garden patio from you. You suggested that he might need sunblinds too. He bought them and you got extra commission !
10. You started your own business.
11. Seeing many jobs needed a driving licence, I saved up & learned to drive.

" *Give me an example of when you showed initiative.* "

Example 12 :

While I was on my month's induction course at my new job with the Tax Office, I realised that MS Outlook would be used extensively and to a sophisticated level. Although I had used email before, such as Yahoo, I did not have those skills and I was going to need them every day .

So, I took the initiative and I asked for training in Outlook. To my surprise, this was refused due to lack of resources. I immediately looked for any online training modules on the inhouse intranet system , found some and asked the IT staff to set me up but was refused on the grounds that I was not to be given full access until my induction was complete. I would be under enough pressure dealing with the public, handling new software, new systems in a new job , with targets without having to stumble through an email system .I wanted to deliver a speedy, high-class service.

I took the initiative again by buying a Teach Yourself Outlook manual and learning the course at the library. I also updated my Windows knowledge and other MS programs skills to deliver the best performance possible. I then had my training assessed and certified.

The result was that my initiative meant that I hit the ground running, delivered a first class-service, gained new certificates and was even being asked by colleagues who had started the same day for help.

Example 13 : I noticed that the customers were forgetting to sign their forms or enclose their money. I suggested the office redesign the flap of the envelopes we sent out, so that they were printed with the words " *Have you signed your form and enclosed your remittance ?*" in bold, letters. My idea saved hundreds of man hours each month.

Example 14 : I worked in the warehouse / storeroom. I noticed that the delivery notes had a superfluous page at the end. It had the company's details on and nothing else. I calculated that it came to a few thousand sheets of wasted paper a year at my location alone. I suggested a redesign of the form. It was adopted nationwide and saved the company £300 per year in stationery.

Example 15 : I got up an hour early every Saturday morning and taught myself to type using an online tutor. It cost me nothing, it took me only 9 weeks to reach a speed of 30 words per minute and got me a job in a solicitor's office. It didn't even wake my baby either as my keyboard is very quiet, unlike a real typewriter ! (typeonline.co.uk or typingclub.com)

"Tell me of a time when you used your initiative " Example 16 :

I had just started in a new job where they did their post manually. After weighing and franking everything, they entered the details into a postbook. One day, when I needed to find something about a Special Delivery postage, while I was online, I happened to notice that we could do our posting online via the Royal Mail site and save a considerable amount of money, £60 per week to be exact.

I took the initiative to read more about it and then to phone them up for more details. I then wrote a short proposal to my manager explaining the situation and outlined how much we were currently paying by posting manually and how much we would save by posting using the Royal Mail online service. I explained that as well as being cheaper, it would also be quicker. I also explained that we could easily print off the details and that he could easily analyse posting costs and volumes at any time via our account.

He objected that we would be in a fix if our IT ever went down and were unable to send our mail, which absolutely had to go out that day. When I reassured him that I had already enquired about that scenario and been told that under those circumstances we could revert back to using our book, providing we attached an explanatory message on the slip, all would be fine. He agreed and told me to set up our account.

The result was that I saved our company over £ 3000 every year and more in man-hours, I was awarded an accolade for my initiative, which was a cash prize of £200.

8.2 The Integrity Competencies

The interviewer wants to know if you fulfilled your obligations and promises; if you were utterly honest and above board in all your dealings; that you treated everyone fairly and consistently; were beyond corruption; that you did what was right.

- I was always honest, open and respectful
- I only ever made realistic, achievable promises and I fulfilled them
- I ensured confidential information remained confidential
- I refrained from gossip and spreading rumours
- I took responsibility for my own actions
- I fulfilled my work commitments
- I behaved ethically and professionally
- I applied all rules fairly
- I behaved consistently
- I was vigilant of all security policies and risks
- I ensured consistency between my communication and my actions
- I knew my limits and sought help when necessary
- I adhered to the organisation's policies

8.2 ex   10 Integrity Examples :

Example 1 : When I worked for the council planning committee , my job was to prepare the reports for the councillors. One day after work, I was approached by a member of the public who tried to bribe me to allow his home extension. He lived in our street and he knew I was a Liverpool fan. He said he had tickets to the Champions League final (which are much rarer than any mere FA Cup final tickets) . I reported the incident in an email. He scored an own goal.

Example 2 : Once when I was in a shop, I was mistakenly given too much change. The cashier gave me change from a £20 note, when actually, I had only given her a £5 note. Instead of dishonestly keeping the money, I told her I had only given her £5. She thanked me for my honesty, saying she would have lost her job, if her till had been short again.

Example 3 : In work, I was told some cruel gossip. I never spread that gossip or confidential information. It later turned out to be untrue and malicious anyway.

Example 4 : When I refereed games or judged talent contests, I always applied rules fairly, even when pressurised. I was fair to everyone, even people I didn't like.

Example 5 : I kept confidential info away from people who tried to access it , such as payroll, marketing people or partners of battered wives trying to locate them to intimidate them.

Example 6 : When I worked in the Stock market and later for the council, I resisted bribes for granting favours and for inside information.

Example 7 : I kept my word at all times and moved heaven and earth to fulfil my promises. I worked weekends to keep my word.

Example 8 : When I was a Team Leader, I did not take credit for or steal the good ideas and suggestions that had been made by other colleagues but gave credit to the idea's rightful owners.

Example 9 : When I worked as a personnel clerk, a friend of a friend , who was a headhunter for a recruitment agency, asked me for some names of senior people in the company that he could poach. I refused.

Example 10 : When I worked in the Immigration Section of the Home Office, I rejected a bribe of £5,000 for an indefinite stay visa and I reported it.

8.3 The Leadership Competencies

The interviewer is looking for evidence that you have led and inspired others by your professionalism, integrity, courage, enthusiasm, fairness, inclusiveness and insistence on quality.

You must show that you are a leader and not merely a manager.

- I accepted responsibility when no one else would

- I took decisive action

- I courageously stepped up to the mark in time of need

- I was a role model by my behaviour : always calm, polite, honest, respectful at all times

- I gained trust from others by being trustworthy, keeping promises

- I maintained strict confidentiality at all times

- I encouraged diversity and used its strengths

- I delegated carefully and appropriately

- I resolved conflicts among colleagues and customers

- I fostered teamwork by encouraging and rewarding cooperation

- I inspired and motivated colleagues by coaching / mentoring them towards their self-development goals

- I led with enthusiasm and personal example, mucking in myself

- I gave myself sufficient technical competence to know what to expect from others

- I was alert to potential risks and problems, either in safety or reputation terms

- I delivered, demanded and assisted colleagues to deliver high quality output / service at all times

- I continually sought to improve myself and the team

- I employed the individual talents of each member to best effect

- I continually sought to cut waste

- I rotated jobs to broaden the experience and development of individuals

- I provided good training

- I valued people (by praising them, being approachable and fair, appreciating their efforts, encouraging and guiding their career)

- I communicated the team's objectives clearly and explained my decisions honestly

- I insisted on quality and improvement all the time

- I got people to achieve more than they thought they could

- I led rather than managed (- leaders make things happen and inspire , whereas managers just administer)

8.3 ex   6 Leadership Examples :

Example 1 : After hearing a colleague maligning our company to a customer, I stressed the importance of company reputation and got to the bottom of the colleague's discontent. I saved our company's reputation from further harm.

Example 2 : When the Team Leader was off sick, I stepped in when no one else would to organise a quick, collaborative meeting in which we all eventually agreed on work duties. I took responsibility and gained the cooperation of others. I efficiently organised the whole team's workload for the day by my action.

Give an example of when you have demonstrated this competency.

Example 3 :

One Monday at the HMRC, our call-centre Team Leader was off sick and no rota or duties had been allocated. Our manager was away at a conference that week. Some staff sat around doing nothing, calls were being missed, things were not good.

I showed leadership by suggesting that we have a short meeting. I asked for two volunteers to man the phones. I reminded everyone that our salary and bonuses were linked to our team targets and that we owed a first class service to the customers anyway. I asked for ideas about the rotas and duties, ensuring everyone got to have a say, including the part-timers, interns and school placement kids.

I maintained team morale with positivity and humour.

There were disputes around who wanted to do what and accusations of cherry-picking. I suggested that we worked to our strengths as much as possible : those who preferred taking the short, easy calls could do that and transfer complex enquiries on to those who preferred the more complex cases or the paperwork cases. I ensured we took into account the early-leaving mothers. My suggestions were adopted.

The outcome was that we met our customer-service targets that week . The customers were happy and we got through it.

I had taken responsibility. By employing the individual skills of each person, fostering inclusion and accounting for the individual diverse needs of people, I had led the team to a peaceful, successful week.

Example 4 : There was an ongoing conflict within our team , which was having an insidious and demoralising effect on everyone. The Team Leader knew about it but seemed unwilling or unable to resolve it and let it drift. I quietly stepped in and resolved it by finding common ground objectives.

Example 5 : When the Area Manager confided in me about his concerns and pleaded with me to be frank, I expressed my frustration that my reported concerns about the lack of quality control on your section were not being addressed. He said that he had been unhappy about our manager for a long time and was unaware about that and he then made the necessary changes. He thanked me for my courage and my insistence on high standards.

In your examples, try to show that you know the difference between a leader and a manager.

Example 6 :

Seeing homeless people sleeping in the doorways outside my work, I took the lead and decided to do something about the problem.

I suggested to our visiting district manager that if staff could raise money by running a relay race between its branches (on a Sunday) , it would involve and bond new staff together and would improve the image of our company, showing it to be socially responsible and committed to the local community. The DM gave the go ahead.

I invited colleagues to vote on which charity we would raise money for (Shelter was chosen) and I enlisted help in all aspects of the planning. I persuaded our other branches within a 20 mile radius to join us, explaining there was a variety of roles needed, not just the runners (- collecting with buckets, giving interviews to the local media, posting photos and info on social media to advertise it, etc). Each branch ran 2 miles then passed the baton on to its sister shop. Our unique selling point was that any of the public could join in and staff could run, walk, skateboard, hoverboard, or pram push the route. We even had panto-horse runners and staff dancing part of their leg, doing the conga.

Everyone had a great time and raised £20,000. The Mayor had been invited to open the race, so we had lots of publicity, pleasing our managers and it led to a promotion and a good pay rise for me.

8.4   The Managing Myself Competencies

The interviewer is looking for evidence that you are your own harshest critic; that you adopt Kaizen, which means constantly looking to improve the efficiency, quality and methods of your work.

- I took responsibility for my performance and targets
- I reviewed and evaluated my work regularly
- I sought and made use of feedback
- I maintained a steady performance
- I sought help with excessive work pressure, if needed
- I remained focused on my objectives
- I prioritized my objectives and schedules
- I understood my development needs
- I sought ways to improve and to expand skills
- I learned from my experiences
- I learned from others
- I took responsibility for developing myself and my career
- I motivated myself to achieve the required outcomes
- I stretched myself, looking for opportunities to develop my role
- I knew the status of my work at all times

8.4   ex   6 Managing Myself Examples :

1. You planned part-time study and childcare around your part-time job

2. You raised kids while holding down a job ! No mean feat !

3. You planned and prioritized your family's resources within a very tight budget

4. You joined evening classes / weekend classes to improve your skills

5. You bought some online courses to improve your skills

6. You taught yourself a new skill or updated your skill via Skype/ Youtube

You can also use some of the 'Initiative ' competency examples for 'Managing Yourself'.

Examples of managing your workload and meeting targets and deadlines are at section 7.5 Deadlines and Targets.

8.5   The Negotiation Competencies

The interviewer wants to see that you have negotiated, not simply threatened to walk away, if your demand was unmet. He wants to hear that you prepared, exchanged views, explored compromises, searched for possible solutions and common ground and found a mutually acceptable agreement.

- I prepared myself in advance and clarified my objectives
- I decided my bottom line in advance
- I prepared how to put my case and gave thought to his likely objectives
- I took a colleague for moral support
- I adopted a positive, polite, professional, collaborative approach
- I explained my view and then let him do most of the talking, to understand his position better
- I actively listened, not interrupting, pre-judging or assuming anything
- I watched his body language to read his expressions and intentions
- I corrected any incorrect statements or omissions or faulty logic with polite questions
- I adjourned to consider his new proposals, if that was necessary
- I looked for a compromise, if needed, by exploring possible solutions
- I encouraged him to discover and embrace alternative perspectives
- I searched for common ground and looked for a win-win situation : the mutual saving of time, costs or waste and the potential mutual achievement of targets
- I was willing to make concessions, if needed, providing they were matched by similar ones in return
- I helped him to recognise the benefits of my concessions
- I secured a satisfactory agreement
- I had the detailed agreement put in writing
- I ensured the agreement included a detailed action plan which of its implementation

From the above, it can be seen that the British government broke every rule in the book, when they were negotiating Brexit with the E.U. – never looking for compromise, never researching the other's views and desires, constantly insulting the EU negotiators and threatening to either walk out or not pay their debts. Shameful and embarrassing. A perfect lesson in how NOT to negotiate from useless idiots.

8.5   ex   12 Negotiation Examples :

1. You negotiated your own salary or pay rise.
2. You negotiated your rent.
3. You negotiated a contract for work that you did or for a job you needed doing for you.
4. You negotiated the sale of a large item - a house or car or similar
5. You negotiated a series of lessons or a course.
6. You haggled over something
7. You bartered - you fixed their computer, they did your garden.
8. You resolved a dispute between people by acting as a negotiator.
9. You negotiated a divorce settlement
10. You negotiated a settlement agreement to give up your job
11. You negotiated to do something for someone in return for something

"Give me an example of when you've negotiated".   **Example 12 :**

I needed to part exchange my car for a new smaller one and saw an advert in the paper offering free road tax for a year as part of the deal on new cars. The ad was for a garage which sold a car I had been researching for weeks.

First of all, I prepared myself by checking the Motorist's Guide to see my car's worth, decided my bottom line and how best to put my case. I took the ad and took a friend for moral support.

At the showroom, I found the model , I explained my situation briefly and let the salesman do most of the talking. When he asked me what part exchange value I wanted, I invited him to make an offer instead. After he examined my car and offered £4,500 , I replied that it was worth at least £6000 because of its condition, regular service history and very low mileage and that I was looking for more than that. I confronted him with the Motorists Guide and my service history.

After he had upped his offer to £ 6000 but refused to go higher, I looked for compromise by exploring possible solutions. I searched for common ground and looked for a win-win situation . I offered to praise him to his HQ for his great customer service , to praise the showroom on several social media sites and drive around with sticker adverts on my car advertising his garage for 6 months. In return, I wanted free servicing for three years, free fog lamps and free air-conditioning. After consulting with his boss, he returned and said I could have two of the three and they liked the social media idea a lot. I agreed. He said I drove a really hard bargain and jokingly said not to come again.

I got the detailed agreement in writing and was I more than happy with the outcome.

8.6   The Persuasion Competencies

The interviewer is looking to see if you have persuaded someone to do something by overcoming their resistance and objections. Perhaps how you have encouraged or motivated someone.

- I researched him, his intentions and objectives.
- I established rapport, mirrored his words & posture
- I took an interest in him
- I made him laugh, endearing him to me
- I flattered him but was careful not to overdo it
- I explained all the benefits and advantages to him
- I used comparisons, examples and stories
- I apologised, making me seem reasonable and honest
- I used repetition
- I urged him not to delay … he'd miss the opportunity
- I offered him an elite, exclusive lifestyle others will envy
- I offered him the chance to be fashionable, in with the in-crowd, a " fashion icon"
- I offered him something that would make him happy or look younger/ sexier / work less / feel free or have more time or money
- I anticipated his resistance and objections
- I introduced peer pressure, telling him all his friends do it or have one
- I used one of his friends or family members to persuade him or confirm
- I told him " You know you want to "
- I encouraged him to imagine the improvements/ how good he would feel
- I told him " You will change your mind. It's inevitable ."
- I extinguished his objections, one by one
- I told him I could see he was already being persuaded
- I supported my points with logic
- I made him feel he was getting something rare
- I quoted the authority of others to support my claims
- I assured him that he had made the right decision
- I facilitated his change

At an interview, you may be asked to tell the difference between convincing , persuading and influencing and to say which is the best.

To **convince** someone of something is to get them to accept your argument by showing them statistics or facts or evidence.

To **persuade** someone to do something is to get them to act in a certain way by appealing to their emotions or their goodness. It might involve flattery or threats.

To **influence** someone is to get them to behave in a certain way and can be through convincing them or persuading them or inspiring them by your behaviour.

It is much better to convince someone than to persuade them. With the latter, they can always change their mind because they haven't been convinced of it, only temporarily swayed.

8.6   ex   16 Persuasion Examples :

1. You persuaded someone to buy something from you.
2. You persuaded someone to buy something for you.
3. You got someone to do something for you, who really didn't want to do it.
4. You got your kids to tidy their rooms. Wow ! ! The job's yours !
5. You persuaded your boss to give you a pay rise
6. You persuaded a colleague to swap his holiday for you.
7. You persuaded someone to change job or house
8. You persuaded your cousin that his friends were bad for him
9. You persuaded someone to give up drink / drugs / cigarettes / overeating.
10. You persuaded someone not to commit suicide.
11. You persuaded someone to donate money.
12. You persuaded someone to play for your team
13. You persuaded someone to volunteer a few hours of their time.
14. You used to run a teenage boys' football team. At first, you couldn't get them to arrive half an hour early for some pre-match practice. When you said there were lots of free sausage rolls for those who came early, they soon conformed.

"Tell me of a time when you persuaded someone to do something"

Example 15 :

My friend had smoked for years and had tried to give up but failed. I started to notice that he was coughing quite a bit. He had already told me that he was spending a fortune on his cigarettes and I was concerned for his health so I decided to try to persuade him to give them up for good.

At first, I started by joking a few times that he sounded like an old man ready for the knacker's yard with that cough. I knew suggesting a visit to the doctor would be futile and he laughed it off. We were good enough friends for me to say that I knew he was spending £60 a week on cigarettes and that I knew a way of both cutting that down to £15 and stopping that bad cough of his. His ears pricked up at the amount he could save and I told him about some e-cigarettes that I had read about.

At first he was apprehensive and scornful, saying they weren't the real thing . I explained that they still had nicotine but reduced amounts so it was healthier. Knowing he liked to be in with the in crowd, I said it's now the fashion. I said I know a place where you can try before you buy and asked if I drove him there, would he try them. He agreed. He was amazed that they came in different flavours too.

The result was that he went onto e-cigs and saved himself a lot of money. More importantly, he took my advice to see a doctor and kept himself healthier.

Example 16 :

When I was a Probation Officer, one of my clients was finding it hard to stay out of prison. He was basically a good person, likeable, funny, gentle and never hurt anyone. He only ever burgled commercial premises, never homes, reasoning that the insurance companies would pick up the tab anyway.

At first, I tried to convince him of the high probability that he would be jailed for quite a long time when he was next caught by showing him some stats and showing him the judge's warning. He understood them but for some reason, they didn't ring his bell.

So, instead, I had to persuade him. I reminded him that he had told me that the most important thing in his life was his mum and how he would do anything for her and how it broke her up whenever he was sent away and how it pained him so much with regret each time he had hurt her. I persuaded him by telling him that whenever he got the urge to put his pirate hat on again, to stop and think about how much pain he would cause his mum.

Thankfully, by saying that and by offering him support to gain qualifications and get interviews with sympathetic employers, I had influenced him to changed his life.

In the above, notice the difference between convincing and persuading. Each has its place. It is horses for courses. Some folk are as daft as a brush or are so suspicious that even when presented with hard, incontrovertible evidence such as confessions or audio recordings or photos or video footage or crystal clear CCTV, they will declare the evidence to be fake. In those cases, persuasion is necessary and you must tap into their emotions, if you wish to change their behaviour.

You might not have been a Probation Officer – I haven't - maybe you were a volunteer adviser of some sort or just a neighbour or good friend or a relative.

8.7 The Problem Solving Competencies

The interviewer wants to hear that you solved a problem in a structured, systematic, scientific manner, rather than in a chaotic, random or lucky way. He wants to hear that you followed a problem-solving model.

He wants to hear how you defined the problem, analysed it and found the solution.

- I defined the problem as accurately as possible
- I identified the relevant info and organised it in a way to help the analysis
- I utilised one of the better problem-solving models (*see below*)
- I analysed the problem illogically, laterally and from different angles
- I checked my assumptions
- I looked for the ' Point of Deviation' from the normal process or system, step by step
- I identified implications, consequences or causal relationships
- I identified hidden patterns or meaning from data or events
- I brainstormed
- I sought assistance, if necessary
- I implemented the solution
- I monitored my solution to ensure the problem had been resolved
- I revised my solution, if necessary
- I took action to prevent the problem recurring

Your problem-solving model must be a methodical, disciplined set of steps :

1. You must DEFINE THE PROBLEM as clearly and precisely as possible. This is often the most important step of all. You must write it out.
2. Try to IDENTIFY THE ROOT CAUSE of it., (thinking logically, then laterally) perhaps using the W5H model for a technical problem (- asking who, what, why, when, where and how) , with particular emphasis on WHEN a problem began occurring (the Point of Deviation). Write them out.
3. You must CONSIDER A RANGE OF POSSIBLE SOLUTIONS, thinking about the pros, cons, risks and potential consequences of each "solution".
4. You must IMPLEMENT your best solution, with a plan and timescale to measure its effectiveness..
5. MONITOR the solution at regular times.
6. ANALYSE THE METRICS Analyse the measurements / results – has your solution worked ? Has the problem been fully resolved ? Does your solution need tweaking or replacing ? If fully resolved, success ! . If not, you must feed another option back into the loop at step 4 or seek assistance from others.

8.7 ex 10 Problem Solving Examples :

1. You fixed a faulty machine, that you had no idea what was wrong with at the start.

2. You fixed a bike/motorbike/car/printer/till-roll.

3. You fixed an annoying noise, which was coming from somewhere in your car. (No, not the backseat driver ☺)

4. You debugged a piece of software code.

5. You cured a computer virus on your PC.

6. You had to fix an Excel spreadsheet but could not at first trace which formula or macro was faulty.

7. You solved a DIY problem at home or on your car.

8. You saw a recurring problem or hazard that you decided to fix.

9. You were working in a very small shop which had a till that you had never seen before. The manager popped out, leaving you alone, the till roll started running out. You looked in the drawer underneath and found another roll but did not know how to change it. It was a really old, unusual type. You looked in the drawer for instructions but found none. So, you phoned the sister store and followed the instructions of their manager by phone.

"Tell me of a time when you have solved a problem at work. "

Example 10 :

When working on a helpdesk in a call-centre, our manager approached me , saying we had dramatically fallen behind our targets for calls answered. Our Team Leader was off sick so she told me to find out what the problem was. My task was to analyse the spreadsheet data for the last few months.

The first thing I did was to define the problem as accurately as possible : in this case, since I knew no one had been off sick, it was that our work was not being recorded accurately for some reason. After I identified the relevant info and organised it in a way to help analysis (breaking it down into months and printing it off), I couldn't see from the raw data what the problem was , so I broke it down further into its constituent parts (into each day).

I analysed our figures logically, using the familiar 'W5H model '(who, what, where, why, when and how) but had no joy. I then approached the problem illogically using lateral thinking and looking at it from different angles but still had no joy.

I checked my assumptions and asked myself "Am I assuming that everyone was entering the data correctly, even though they were experienced staff ? " Therefore, I looked for the 'Point of Deviation from the System' , step by step and then I found what the problem was - the number of calls recorded had dropped dramatically in the first few days of the New Year 2012 because some of the staff had been incorrectly entering the old year as 2011. They had been inserting the correct day and month but had still mentally been attuned to the 2011 and so the calls were being incorrectly totalled.

I suggested to my manager that we adopt a formula on the spreadsheet to write the date instead of manually typing it ourselves each morning and she agreed. The moral is perhaps not to take things at face value or make assumptions.

In an interview, be sure to say that you used a problem-solving model to solve your problem. If you don't, you will probably fail.

The common problem solving models are :

The **W5H model** – This is best used to resolve a technical problem such as when a mechanical process has stopped functioning . You must ask <u>W</u>ho, <u>w</u>hat, <u>w</u>hy, <u>w</u>hen, <u>w</u>here and <u>h</u>ow , with particular emphasis on WHEN a problem began occurring , the Point of Deviation.

MAPPING - Using a Spider map / Mindmap / Fishbone map – This is best used when you need to generate new ideas. You write down the problem at one point and then write out possible solutions to branch off that.

S.W.O.T   analysis – is used when the problem involves a challenge or threat from a competitor. You write down the **S**trengths, **W**eakneseses, **O**pportunities and **T**hreats that the challenge poses to both sides.

FIELD FORCE analysis - This is your simple Pros –v Cons list and is best used when you are sure there are only two options. You list the pros (advantages) and cons (disadvantages) of each course of action.

COST-BENEFIT analysis - is a very precise examination of a course of action to justify its adoption in terms of cost. In order for it to be compelling, it has to be   (a) logical (b) be financially sound (best if you can say that you've had the finance department back you up on that) and (c) it has to be operationally coherent, credible and workable.

The other problem-solving solving techniques (such as brain-storming, lateral thinking or De Bono's 'Hats' methods are best not used as examples).

8.8   The Teamworking Competencies

The interviewer is trying to determine ways in which you have contributed to the success of a team or if you have acted selfishly. He wants to see that you pull your weight, respect the skills and views of colleagues, share info and put the team's goal above your own.

- I was friendly, helpful and approachable
- I valued the diverse perspectives, skills, experience, talents and needs of my colleagues
- I shared my ideas and relevant knowledge
- I showed interest in the opinions of others
- I placed the common group goal above my own goals
- I co-operated with customers, internal and external team members, stake-holders
- I pulled my weight in the team.
- I supported my colleagues with their workload, when I could
- I praised my colleagues when they were successful
- I sought opportunities for cross-functional working and collaboration
- I was flexible over shifts, duties and holidays
- I learned the role of others in the team(s), so as to work better together
- I accepted responsibility for my work
- I employed the diversity of the team to assist me
- I participated in team meetings and post-mortems
- I accepted feedback from colleagues on how I impacted on others
- I was always willing to compromise
- I treated all my colleagues with respect at all times
- I was patient, tolerant, didn't play the blame game or gossip
- I maintained team morale with positivity, enthusiasm and humour
- I offered only gentle constructive feedback
- I balanced my own needs with those of the team
- I knew T.E.A.M. means Together Everyone Achieves More
- I knew that there is no " I" in TEAM.

8.8ex   22 Teamworking Examples :

1. You worked in team
2. You played in a sports team
3. You worked on a project in school that required teamwork. Perhaps a Geography or Science project or coursework.
4. You shared information with others in the team
5. You offered to help others in the team when you had finished your work
6. You improved team morale with humour
7. You worked with neighbours to clear snow or litter
8. You contributed to a team in your church
9. You participated in a Parent-Teacher forum
10. You worked in a team in your hobby group competing against other towns. Chess team ? Footy team ? Brass band ? Choir ?
11. You participated in a team when you were sent on a course
12. You resolved conflict within a team
13. You stayed longer after work to help a colleague
14. You did more than your allocation of work
15. You served on a jury
16. You swapped your day off or holidays to help a team colleague
17. You played in a band or sang in a choir
18. You showed flexibility over shifts
19. At your foodbank or neighbourhood watch scheme, you typed and printed the menus or typed the minutes.

When writing your answer, choose an example from your Experiences Autobiography which most closely matches the duties of the job in the advert.

Be sure to include some of the competency indicators mentioned in 8.8

" *Tell me about a time when you worked in a team* "....

Example 20 :

There was a time when I was called upon to do jury service. The group was quite diverse in many ways . It ranged in ages from about 20 to about 65, from all socio-economic backgrounds, from various races, colour and religions. I thought it would be interesting to see if everyone would work together.

For my part, what I did was I respected and valued the diverse views, perspectives and experience of all the other members. Whenever I gave feedback about their suggestions and ideas , it was always gentle and positive. Similarly, I respected and accepted the feedback from fellow team-members about my suggestions and observations. I praised their good suggestions. I employed the diversity of the group to assist my understanding.

I contributed to the team by sharing my knowledge and ideas and I contributed to the team morale with humour and enthusiasm. We could not agree upon a unanimous verdict and so were ordered to reconsider . When we were still unable to reach a 10 to 2 verdict, were again told to go back until we did. By this stage, some tempers were getting frayed. Some people were just wanting to go home. I resolved disputes and conflict among team-members who argued, by finding common ground and seeing that contradictory views are sometimes just misunderstandings and misinformation. That helped and we finally reached a 10 to 2 majority verdict which the judge accepted.

The result was that I facilitated in playing a part in ensuring justice was done as much as possible. I had helped a diverse group to work together as a team. I had gained valuable experience from the event, by working with such a diverse group and it later stood me in good stead, as it helped me get a better job.

He included **some** competency **indicators of Teamwork** : I respected and valued diverse views, of others..... gave gentle and positive feedback...praised their good suggestions... employed the diversity of the group to assist me ...contributed to the team by sharing my knowledge and ideas ... contributed to the team morale with humour and enthusiasm... resolved disputes by finding common ground.

Example 21 :

A colleague was to return to work on the coming Monday after a long absence. There had been major upgrades to our software and changes around the office. Our Team Leader was still off sick and that our manager would be away on a conference, so I determined to assist my colleague's return to work as best I could.

That day, Friday, I retrieved my notes from the last 6 months and photocopied only the ones I thought to be essential . I then stocked up my colleague's stationery drawer with the current new stationery. I contacted our I.T guru and ensured that her PC had been upgraded and was ready to rock.

When my colleague returned, I warmly and sensitively welcomed her back. I informed her of the changes she would need to know about immediately, without overloading her and briefly walked her through the new interface. I assured her that I would be there for any help she needed and that there was no such thing as a stupid question.

I took my lunch break to coincide with her's and kept a discreet eye on her, helping her in a quiet, unobtrusive way, when I saw her queue of customers building up excessively.

The outcome was that she told my manager that she would never have got through the day without my actions and that she wished everyone was as good a team worker as I was. My manager thanked me, both then and in my appraisal.

Example 22 :

When at my local surgery, I noticed a poster which invited local people to join a Patient Participation Group. Thinking this might be useful to me in a number of ways, I copied down the website and investigated it when I got home.

After reading the details,I decided to join and persuaded two of my friends to do likewise, seeing it as a platform to promote the needs and views of my age group in local health planning matters and also seeing it as a way of gaining experiences for my CV.

I and my friends were made very welcome, since our age group had been very under-represented in the consultation and planning. Once a month, we met with all sorts of health professionals and gave our views and those of all our friends, whom we had canvassed for their opinions and ideas.

In the course of those meetings,I gained a lot of confidence in the areas of communication and teamwork. I learned about respecting the needs and viewpoints of others in the group, how to work alongside people of different ages and cultural backgrounds, how to collaborate and co-operate with people who differed in terms of ability, sexuality, race and health needs.

My experience in the group was a maturing one, I made some good friends and it helped me get a new job by being able to provide an example of real life experience of teamwork.

Chapter 9   Action Words to Use

When writing your answers and when in the interview, use these words to describe the actions you took :

I achieved
I adapted
I adopted
I analysed
I arranged
I assessed
I built
I combined
I compiled
I completed
I conducted
I controlled
I considered
I consulted
I coordinated
I created
I delivered
I designed
I developed
I devised
I diagnosed
I directed
I eliminated
I enabled
I encouraged
I ensured
I established
I exceeded
I expanded
I extracted
I evaluated
I evolved
I fostered
I furthered
I gained
I gathered
I generated
I identified
I implemented
I improved
I initiated
I increased
I influenced
I instigated
I integrated
I introduced

I launched
I led
I liaised
I managed
I minimised
I monitored
I motivated
I negotiated
I offered
I organised
I perfected
I performed
I persevered
I persuaded
I planned
I pre-empted
I prepared
I prioritized
I produced
I progressed
I promoted
I proposed
I queried
I quantified
I raised
I recovered
I redesigned
I reorganised
I rescheduled
I resolved
I restored
I saved
I secured
I simplified
I solved
I streamlined
I strengthened
I suggested
I trained
I transformed
I volunteered

Chapter 10 The interview

10.1 There are bad interviewers Be ready for bad interviewers. Some will constantly interrupt you while you are narrating your example but don't let that throw you. Stay calm. Be sure you can back up what you have said. They may probe you for more in-depth details or for clarification.

10.2 Recognizing the questions Part of the skill in handling competency questions is recognizing what an interviewer actually wants from you. Thankfully, most questions will be straightforward. If an interviewer wishes to know how you have adapted to changes in working practices, he will usually say something like : " *We are a fast-moving environment here with many shifting demands and we expect our staff to be flexible to those demands. Can you give me an example of when you have had to cope with such changes ?"* However, some questions will not be so clear cut . Their question will be indirect and oblique. If you are unsure in any way as to what you are being asked, it is **vital** that you ask. It is no use to anyone if you narrate a competency example which is not the one which was required.

10.3 They may take notes One of the interviewers may well be taking notes as you answer. Don't be phased by this at all : in fact, see this in a very positive light The more they write down, the more they like what they are hearing; the more key indicators you can include in your story, the more you will be demonstrating that you meet the competency. If you see them taking lots of notes, it's a very good sign but don't ramble on !

10.4 Silences and feedback After you have given your example, don't be tempted to waffle to fill any awkward silence. Don't expect immediate feedback , either verbal or in the form of smiles or nods. Have faith and keep stumm. . If you have prepared well, you already have a massive advantage over those who have not bothered and there will be many like that.

10.5 You can refer to your notes You can take your scripts to the interview as reminders but you can't read them all the way through ! The interviewers will not mind you glancing occasionally at bullet points or headings you have highlighted to remind yourself. Your interview is not a memory test and they will not expect you remember everything.

10.6 If you can't think of an example

If you struggle to remember an example, firstly, **play for time**. Ask the interviewer to give you a moment to think or ask if you can come back to that question later. That will not count against you in any way.

Secondly, realise that your experiences serve several masters and can be used for several competency answers. **Competencies overlap**. When you are delivering excellent customer service, you are also communicating well, so that could be used to answer two competency questions.

The example given for ' Adapting to Change in Chapter 5, could also be used for Initiative, if you were on the spot and could not think of anything. Examples for Communication can often be used for Customer Service and vice versa. An example given for Deadlines can often also be used as an example of Managing Yourself.

The example of Negotiation could be used for Persuasion, if you were really on the spot and could not think of any other example.

" **Tell me about your biggest achievement** " is a very common question. Don't be surprised if you get asked it. If you are, then your answer can come from any of these competencies : Deadlines and Targets, Drive, Determination . Resilience, Initiative, Negotiation or Problem Solving.

Thirdly, **use your imagination**. Remember your long-forgotten uncle who had a small business. Yes, him. I'm sure you can remember him if you want the job badly enough.

10.7 Appear natural

Although you will have rehearsed your stories many times, make it appear as though you have thought them up on the spot and not rehearsed them. You need to appear as though you are fully competent at your job and do it effortlessly.

10.8 Give them an example, even if they don't ask for one

Because you have taken the trouble to read so far in this book, I am now going to reveal to you one of the most powerful techniques for getting a job. Always answer the interviewer with an example. In other words, give the interviewer an example of what you've done, even if he didn't ask you for it. If he asks you "Have you ever handled cash ?" Don't just say "Yes I have " . You must say "Yes I have and I was penny perfect. When I worked at XXXX, I won the cashier of the month award five times." If he asks "Have you ever been a keyholder ?", don't just say "Yes I have". Say "Yes I have and I was not only entrusted with all the office keys but I was on call too" Or " I was also entrusted with the spare master key". **Always answer with an example**, even if you are not asked for an example. After I began to tell my jobseekers to do that, the results were stratospheric. It is one of the most potent secrets to getting a job. Always, always, always answer the interviewer's question with an example of how you have already done that or something similar, even, if he didn't ask you for an example. Remember that : It is worth its weight in gold.

10.9   Heed the usual interview protocols :

Take yourself there early. Check the location in advance using Google Maps or similar and the transport. Even make a dummy run. Arriving early will allow you some last-minute revision of your notes. Get there early and revise your CV and answers. It pays off.

Take your smart clothes. Dress smartly. If you are wearing something for the first time, such as a new shirt, wash it first so that you feel comfortable in it.

Take your scripts / notes and CV. ...to look through beforehand.

Take the right attitude. Have the attitude that the interview is just a chat about a possible job. Think to yourself : "It *is not really an interview, **it's just a CHAT**. I'll be offered the job because I've put more work and preparation in than the other candidates. It's a mere formality. I'm not nervous because it's not an interview - it's a chat.* "

Many jobseekers have told me that the advice of seeing the meeting as a "chat" rather than an interview, was really effective in dissolving their nervousness. They also report that believing that they **already had the job** gave them great confidence. Take the right attitude. Confident but not arrogant.

If you can remember only one thing , then remember this : tell them you have already done the job - or something very similar to it - in some way.

If you have prepared your examples and rehearsed them well, you will be raring to demonstrate them. Many other candidates just can't be bothered. You can. That's what makes the difference.

Chapter 11 Competency Options tests

The application process for some jobs involves your having to complete a Competency Options test. In this, you are given a situation and told to rank four given responses, which most closely matched the behaviour you exhibited in that situation.

For example, in a CUSTOMER SERVICE situation, you are told to think of a time when you dealt with a customer who was very demanding in terms of the time, advice and amount of help they wanted from you. You are told to rank these four responses in order from 1 to 4, with 1 being the response you took and 4 being the least likely you would have taken :

A ... I began with the intention of treating everyone equally but I found that I liked some people more than others and I admit that I was more likely to help those more.

B ... I can't pretend that I treated everyone the same. The ones who were undeserving and had bad attitudes got the bare service from me.

C ... I tried to be always fair and helpful but I must admit that how I treated people varied with how they treated me and how I felt on the day.

D ... I ensured that I was as fair as could be and that everyone received the same treatment , no matter how I felt personally.

The best way to tackle these is to firstly **look for the worst response** : in other words, the response that you would certainly NOT have done and to mark it as number 4. So here, I think you will agree that the poorest example of delivering customer service is option B. Naturally, someone working in a customer service role cannot decide to give the " bare service" to their customers, just because the customers are being demanding or " undeserving " !

The next step is to identify the response that you would have taken. Here, it is option D. So, you mark that as number 1. You gave your best service to every customer, regardless of how difficult and demanding they were.

That is the strategy that you must always adopt : firstly identify the worst response because usually it is the easiest to decide and assign it to number 4. Then secondly, identify the best response and assign it to number 1. The remaining two options usually have only a very subtle difference between them and it is not too important in which order you place these. I would assign the second best response to A and the third to C. Final answer ....1-D, 2-A, 3-C, 4-B.

Another example ... TEAMWORK..... You worked in a team and are told to rank these in order.

A ... When I worked with others, I valued the differences between us and that each person had something different to contribute.

B ... I found it difficult working with people who were different from me because you need people with more similarities than differences.

C ... I appreciate that people were entitled to be different from me and I tried to adjust to their different ways.

D ... I was quite uncomfortable if they were different from me and found it difficult to adjust to their different ways of thinking.

Again, follow the strategy .. **look for the WORST** option.......look for what you would NOT have done or said and mark that as number 4 ......

I think you will agree that the worst option has to be the last one . **Now, look for the best** one and mark it as number 1 .... I think you will agree that it has to be the first one in the list above : he " valued " the differences, whereas the third option only tried to adjust . I would now suggest that C is better than B and so C comes second.. Final answer = 1-A, 2-C,3-B, D-4.

Another example .... ACCURACY ....You had to maintain accuracy in your work. Rank these in order of how you normally behaved.

A ... I didn't check my work, as people were generally satisfied with it.

B - I spent almost as much time checking my time as I did doing it.

C - I checked those parts where errors could most easily creep in.

D ... I always checked my work , though as I grew in experience and confidence, I was able to spend less and less time on this.

Following the strategy, you look for the worst option and assign it to number 4. Then find the best option, that is, the one that you actually did and assign that to option number 1. Then decide the better of the remaining two and assign it to number 2.

The final answer is 1-D, 2-C, 3-B, 4-A

A is clearly the worst. It shows idleness, complacency and arrogance. B is the next worst . At least this person checks their wok but the employer would not recruit someone so incompetent. Of the remaining two, C is the poorer because errors can creep into any area of our work, not just the parts we expect.

The clever way to tackle these is to do them with friends and to share your thoughts. Two heads are better than one and five heads are better than two.

Don't fuss too much about the inner answers. It is the first and last in the ranks that you must get right.

Finally, before you submit your answers, recheck that you have written them in the correct order. It is very easy to record them incorrectly.

Chapter 12   After the interview and beyond

If you don't get that particular job

The secret in getting a good job is knowing the right thing to do, doing it and persisting in doing it until you are successful. When you have been rejected for a position, it can be for many reasons. You might have demonstrated your competencies perfectly but the employer felt that you would not fit into the culture of his company or that team for whatever reason. Sometimes, an employer will withdraw a vacancy after the interviews. It does happen . It could be that you were considered excellent but one candidate had slightly more experience than you. It is common for six candidates to be invited for an interview . Four might have scored less than 80 %. You might have scored 96 % but the winner scored 96.5%. Since you don't know how close you came to landing that job, you will feel that you are a failure and that you will never master these competency interviews and that you will never get the job you want. Sadly, this is what we tend to do. We think the worst. We catastrophise.

Examine how you performed and be honest. If you felt that you performed badly on any examples, ask yourself why. Did you need better examples ? Did you need more examples ? Did you need more practice ? If you were prodded for more details, were you able to give the specific detail that was wanted ?

What is important is that you move on and persist.

By constructing an Experiences Autobiography, you are doing the right thing. By constructing and learning your scripts according to the model I have given, you are giving the employer examples of the key indicators of the competencies he is seeking. You are doing the right thing and on the right track. The final unit is for you to show perseverance. You will succeed if you persevere. The formula works and you will win when the conditions and time are right.

What also counts is the time and effort you have expended in remembering all your experiences. Go back through your Autobiography and cross-check it with the key indicators given in chapters 7 and 8 and examples suggested underneath them. If you have very few experiences and examples and are really desperate, think of experiences of your brothers and sisters and friends.

Keep updating your Experiences Autobiography !

You must constantly keep adding to your Autobiography with examples of your behaviours. If you are currently working, stay alert to how you are contributing to your team for examples of Teamwork. If you work in a Customer Services environment, record examples of how you have delivered excellent service and how maybe dealt with demanding customers and complaints. Simply spend 10 or 15 minutes at the end of each working day recording what you did that day.

It's easy if you travel by train or bus to jot it down in your diary or record it into your phone or mp3 voice recorder. Make it a daily habit of forcing yourself to briefly skim through all the competencies and note down any examples. Then some time later, you can expand them into scripts. I cannot emphasise this enough ! ! !

When you get the job - and you will, sooner or later...

When you get the job - You will, sooner or later. When you get that email or letter and you have calmed down after all the excitement, Congratulations ! Go out and treat yourself.! **Finally...If you have found this book helpful PLEASE be so kind and give it a good rating on Amazon**. You might also wish to buy another copy to give to someone you know, who is looking for work or to change their job.

If applying for a Civil Service job, you will need my other book The Civil Service Competencies Book for Job Interviews. (Some of the material in this book also appears in that one). See the next page for details.

Search Amazon books for 'Mike New' You won't regret it. You know you will do it anyway. ☺

Thank you. I wish you good luck and all good things in life.Mike

If you are applying for a job within the Civil Service, you will find that they have their own set of competencies, quite unlike the mainstream ones used by most employers. The best thing that you can do is to buy >>>

The Civil Service Competencies Book

2nd edition revised and expanded

By Mike New

It includes detailed advice and examples on :

Competency 1 'Seeing the big picture'

Competency 2 'Changing and Improving'

Competency 3 'Making effective decisions'

Competency 4 'Leading and communicating'

Competency 5 'Collaborating and partnering'

Competency 6 'Building capability for all'

Competency 7 'Achieving commercial outcomes'

Competency 8 'Delivering value for money'

Competency 9 'Managing a quality service'

Competency 10 'Delivering at pace'

Available now on Amazon   Some of the material in that book also appears in this one.

Printed in Great
Britain
by Amazon

31471438R00068